LIFE**ABUNDANT**365!

DON DAY

I dedicate this book to my Lord and Savior, Jesus Christ,
for without Him there would be no Abundant Life.

CONTENTS

INTRODUCTION

LIVING AN UNCOMMON LIFE is the cure for a common life. I'm talking about a life of abundance. An extraordinary life you can experience 365 days a year.

An abundant life is about more than material things. Find love, joy, peace, and the rest of the fruits of the Spirit and eternal life and you will truly have an abundant life. We all have a wheel—I'll call "Equities of Life"—that includes professional life, personal life, physical life, financial life, and spiritual life. To live an Abundant Life 365, you must be successful in every area of your life. This book will motivate, inform, inspire, and transform you into a person of happiness and joy, leading you to an Abundant Life 365!

No particular order must be followed to benefit from this book. Each chapter brings a different message. You'll notice that I harp on some of the same topics and messages in multiple chapters in the book. The idea is not to be repetitive, rather to remind you about important thoughts within this book.

I want to help you rekindle your dreams and show you they're not only possible, but also attainable, even now. I want to show you the path that will lead you directly and expeditiously to them. I also want to help you answer some life-changing questions. What's your ultimate purpose? What really motivates and ignites your passion? What will keep that passion burning long enough for you to achieve your wildest, most outrageous goals?

I suggest you begin this book along with a journal. Make notes and write your thoughts as you take this journey to abundant living. This trip will take you through the streets and alleyways of every area of your life. The journal will hold your thoughts, dreams, needs, and emotions. This book is not academic theory, but sixty years of real-life experience that works whenever and wherever applied.

Ready? Here we go!

CHAPTER ONE:
Share Your Story

You, Lord, will keep the needy safe and will protect us forever from the wicked, who freely strut about when what is vile is honored by the human race. —Psalm 12:7-8 NIV

OUR WORLD IS DIVIDED AND MESSY. Political correctness has become more important than biblical correctness. Many beliefs, habits, religions, and traditions are all around us, leaving us feeling unqualified, or unable, to effectively share our beliefs. Rest assured that you are well equipped to make a difference in your little spot of the world. If you don't share your beliefs and experiences, we are but two generations away from losing it all. Tell the next generation. Share your story with your family, children, and grandchildren. Help them understand.

You will feel satisfied once you share your story with those over whom you have influence. After all, it's your story and it's not up for debate.

Make yourself available, and then start small. Take one step at a time and follow the still quiet voice of the Lord, the God of Abraham, Isaac, and Jacob. Opportunities will come to you and you can help others. Stop getting ready to do something. Do it already! Your life will improve because you serve others. That's abundance! Keep going!

DIG DEEP:

Have you held back from sharing your story because you're afraid of rejection or appearing to be better than others? Are you concerned that you'll be rejected or embarrassed? Look, it's your story and not open for debate. People welcome your story and they are drawn closer to you by hearing your story. My rule has always been: What other people think of you is none of your business! So, just do it!

CHAPTER TWO:
Three Words That Will Change Your Life

GET-OVER-IT!

We've all had things that caused us sadness, diminishment, anger, distress, and every other emotion known to man. Life is messy and unfair. By hanging on to unforgiveness and anger, we are doomed to live a life of deficit, not abundance. Our past can define our future if we don't get over it and move forward. Just take the next step.

A woman once gave her husband the silent treatment for two days only to find out he wasn't even aware—and she had been working hard at ignoring him. Talk about mixed messages! Her husband figured they were getting along famously. After all, she wasn't complaining, correcting, or fighting with him. Point being: Failing to get over it usually harms you far more than anyone else.

I'm not inviting you to position yourself for additional abuse or problems with someone from your past. I'm simply suggesting you forgive—get over it—and move on with your future.

Don't let the past keep you from your potential. Forgive and forget and get over it! This will change your life for the better and forever. Just ask yourself: what will matter to you fifty years from today?

You can only control you. You're 100 percent responsible for your actions. Whatever you're hanging on to—get over it!

DIG DEEP:

Are there things in your life that you need to get over? Are you harboring resentment or holding something against someone that keeps you from moving forward? No matter what happened, or how unfair, why not make today the day you get over it and move on with your life? This is the direction to LifeAbundant365.

CHAPTER THREE:
Habits Are 100 Times Stronger than Desires

"We are what we repeatedly do." —Aristotle

WE FORM HABITS FOR TWO REASONS: First, to avoid pain. Second, to receive pleasure.

Over time, these actions will help you form strong habits. Habits that you will perform unconsciously. Forty percent of our actions are done without thinking. Have you ever driven your car somewhere and upon arrival, you didn't remember driving there? Physically you were there, but in your mind, you were somewhere else. You were operating on autopilot. Operating out of habit. We've all done it. Habits control our lives.

Small habits are transforming you every day—right now!

Without change, the second half of our life is made up of the habits/beliefs/values we accumulated during the first half. Remember: You will never change your life until you change something you do daily. The secret to your success can be found in your daily routine.

Good habits include:

- Practice being powerfully present.
- Stop trying to be interesting and become interested.

- Visualize: Success is an inside-out process.
- Your mind eavesdrops on your self-talk. Think good thoughts.
- Control the first and last hours of your day.

DIG DEEP:

Are you trying to get through the day, or get something from the day? So many of us run on autopilot and fail to be present in our lives. We are reacting to circumstances and challenges, not responding. Why? Our habits. To break a habit requires identification of that habit, discipline, and consistency. Review your daily routine and define where your habits are taking you. Identify your bad habits and replace them with good habits. Over time the good habits will take over and get you closer to where you really want to be without you knowing it—autopilot. This is LifeAbundant365.

CHAPTER FOUR:

All Things Through Him ...

I can do all things through Him who strengthens me. —*Philippians 4:13*

WHAT IF WE REALLY BELIEVED THAT? In your mind and heart, you know that you can do all things through Him who strengthens you. You can do all things! What if you were told every day of your life that you could, and can do, all things until you finally believed it? How would your life be different? How would your self-confidence be?

> I can do all things through Him who strengthens me.
> —Philippians 4:13

With this powerful statement, along with a little self-belief, you can be almost bulletproof. Confidence drives you to take calculated risks.

You may not be the best at everything you attempt, and who is great when they first try anything new? But you can do all things, so just do it!

Encourage others that they can do all things. Brand into your children that they can do all things. Then watch lives change and live in abundance!

Excelling at anything is all about repetition. You have to put in the reps! You are what you repeatedly do. Repeat to yourself every day and throughout the day, "I can do all things through Him who gives me strength." Put in the reps. Eventually it will become a habit and second nature, and thus, it will become your belief. Every time a challenge comes, you will say, "I can do all things!"

DIG DEEP:

Where have you convinced yourself that you can't do something? What negative talk do you tell yourself without thinking? Imagine what will occur when you begin to believe that you can do all things. Your life conditions will change when you do. Just take the first step.

CHAPTER FIVE:
Love Thyself!

HAVING BEEN AROUND PEOPLE for the past sixty years, I've grown certain about many things. Among them: People love themselves.

All of us could write a book titled: *I'm Not Much, but I'm All I Ever Think About!* Chapter One: ME, Chapter Two: MORE ABOUT ME, Chapter Three: NOW YOU TALK ABOUT ME! ME-ME-ME!

To illustrate my belief, think about a group picture you were in. When you got to review the picture, who did you look for first? Yourself, right? If you look good, it's a good picture. If not, it's a bad picture. We love ourselves, and because we love ourselves, we should exercise caution.

Close friends are needed to live LifeAbundant365. You don't gain or maintain friendships by talking only about yourself! You must encourage others to tell you about them, then shush! People will gladly share all things them and they will like you better for asking them to do so! All you have to do is listen to their story. Ask them questions about their life and show sincere interest. You will be special to them because showing such interest in someone else is unusual. All because you love yourself enough that you don't have to be the center of your attention.

Having true and great relationships with others creates a great beginning for living a life abundant! At the end of our lives, it's family and friends that matter the most to us. This is a big part of life fulfillment! No regrets!

DIG DEEP:

How do people in your life see you around other people? How do you act when meeting someone for the first time? Where do you focus your energy when in a group? Do you try to be interesting or gain attention or do you shine the light on others? Living LifeAbundant365 means having a lot of friends with whom to share your life. Not just acquaintances. Real friends. Try this today. When you're introduced to someone new, become sincerely interested in him or her and not yourself.

CHAPTER SIX:
No Excuses!

"A person who is good at excuses is seldom good at anything else." —*Benjamin Franklin*

EXCUSES CAN, AND DO, become limiting beliefs. The more you excuse, the more it becomes a part of you and opens the exit door from your potential.

Why are some people more successful than others? Why do some people make more money, live happier lives, and accomplish much more in the same number of years than the great majority? Why haven't you reached your potential up until now?

What you say next will determine if you are making excuses or have accepted responsibility for your life!

The problem with most of our list of "why we haven't accomplished more" is that we don't have "us" listed as the reason for not reaching "our" potential!

Excuses will diminish you, and they largely are the same:

"I didn't have a happy childhood."

"I didn't get a good education."

"I don't have any money."

"My boss is really critical."

"My marriage is no good."

"No one appreciates me."

"The economy is terrible."

Sound familiar?

> A person who is good at excuses
> is seldom good at anything else.
> —Benjamin Franklin

Making excuses isn't anything new. Consider the following scripture:

The man said, "The woman whom you gave to be with me, she gave me fruit of the tree, and I ate." —Genesis 3:12 (ESV)

Then the Lord God said to the woman, "What is this that you have done?" The woman said, "The serpent deceived me, and I ate." —Genesis 3:13 (ESV)

We come by excuses honestly! Think about what Adam and Eve said above. That didn't work out so well, did it?

Repeat after me: "This year I will not take, and I will not make, excuses!"

To live a life of no excuses, you must:

- Decide to not make excuses!
- Do what you already know to do.
- Start with what's next. What do you want and what's the first thing you have to do to get started? Then do it!
- Never have a great idea that you know you should do and not take the next step toward doing it.
- Always take responsibility and action for your life conditions.

DIG DEEP:

Reflect over your life and think of the times when you made excuses for your failures, shortcomings, or lackluster performances. No doubt, there have been seasons in your life when you played the victim card when you should have been taking responsibility for how you responded to your challenge or circumstance. Remember, ideas without action are worthless. In the end it's all up to you. Today is the day you need to move ahead. No more excuses!

CHAPTER SEVEN:
No Regrets

LOOKING IN THE REARVIEW MIRROR, I can vividly see areas of my life that I regret, though my regrets are not the usual suspects.

I've traveled extensively, jumped out of airplanes, completed endurance races, owned companies, and taken great risks with great rewards. I'm blessed to have written books, to have shared at my speaking events, and to have brokered real estate deals every day.

My regrets stem more from not loving enough. Not being there for my children when they were very young. Not telling my friends how much I loved them and how much they mean to me. Not hugging enough and not being there for those who needed me the most. I regret every time I told others and myself my excuse—"I was doing it for my family"—when my family would prefer me to be with them.

I've changed during the past decade. I've made the effort to put the needs of others before my own. I tell friends how much I love them and value our relationship. I attend basketball games, dance recitals, swim lessons, and soccer games with my grandchildren. I play hide-and-seek, cards, and laugh now more than ever.

A 2010 Harvard study revealed that up to 90 percent of Americans have a major regret, or regrets, in their lives. What are your regrets?

Here are the top regrets for most:

- Not traveling more.
- Not being true to yourself. (Living for others and their expectations.)
- Not learning more (education training experiences).
- Not spending more time with family and friends.
- Not following your inner voice, your path, your passion. (Fear)
- Not loving others more fully. Not letting them know!

Inaction is the most devastating regret!

You will have memories. What will they be?

We can't change the past but we can sure do something about the future.

> *Brothers, I do not consider that I have made it my own. But one thing I do: forgetting what lies behind and straining forward to what lies ahead, I press on toward the goal for the prize of the upward call of God in Christ Jesus. —Philippians 3:13*

I haven't figured it all out, but now I "Live–Love–Laugh" every day. I order as follows: God first, my wife second, my children third, and my grandkids next.

My friends know I love and value them. My wife, Shelly, will say, "Would you like to go to dinner with … " And I'll answer "Yes" before she announces their names. I love people.

My past doesn't define me, though it has prepared me to live a life with no regrets and so can you. Now that's LifeAbundant365!

DIG DEEP:

Each of us would like a "do over" for something in our past. We've all said or done things we wished we hadn't. We can't change what's happened, but we can adjust our sails and head in a new direction. Where do you need an adjustment in your sails? What must you do to reduce the regrets for the future?

CHAPTER EIGHT:
Filling Your Tank!

Therefore, we do not lose heart, but though our outer man is decaying, yet our inner man is being renewed day by day. —2 Corinthians, 4:16

TO SAY MY FATHER WAS 'FRUGAL" would be an understatement.

Dad thought everything was too expensive—didn't matter what it was, food, cars, fuel, homes, clothes, etc.—and he made sure everyone knew how he felt.

If someone called long distance, Dad would lose his mind. "Get in here, your aunt wants to talk with you—and it's long distance!"

Dad created ways to save money.

Later, when we'd go to my parents' home while on vacation, he'd tell us at the end of the visit just before we left: "When you get home, call us collect and ask for Julie. We'll say, 'Julie's not here' and hang up. That will be the code you made it home safely."

Total savings: 17 cents.

Frugalness ran in Dad's family. Being true to that nature was his way of keeping his tank full. How about you?

What fuels your tank in life?

- Physical: Work out, run, weights, sports, diet, nutrition.
- Family: Goals, training, relationships, growth, trust.
- Personal (what brings you joy): Happiness/passion.
- Professional: Goals, plans, vision, hustle, work, finance, savings, motivation.
- Spiritual: Church, Bible reading, study, prayer.

You must stay motivated, which is true for many things in life. You can't just flip a switch and suddenly you're changed for life. Most meaningful and important things require persistence and effort.

We are all human, so we leak.

What drains your tank?

- Professional: Management, clients, deadlines, co-workers, staff …
- Physical: Lack of exercise, poor health, injuries, diets.
- Personal: Not enough free time, attitude, not knowing what you want, trying to get through the day, not get something from the day.
- Spiritual: Unbelief, self-control.
- Family: Money, spouse, children, bills …

We know what fills our tank, but when we get busy, we tend to quit filling it. If our tank is low, we operate less efficiently and we are prone to make more mistakes.

DIG DEEP:

Life requires our best. The one constant to live LifeAbundant365 is to fill our tank with the good things in every area of our life. It's easy to do and it's easy not to do. In what areas of your life are you leaking? Take time to evaluate the leaks in your tank and find what you need to refill them with the good stuff.

CHAPTER NINE:
The Nitty-Gritty!

The way is hard that leads to life. —*Matthew 7:14*

By your endurance you will gain your lives. —*Luke 21:19*

ON MY FIFTIETH BIRTHDAY, I ran an ultramarathon 50-mile race. Around the 34-mile marker, I caught up to a younger runner who had a nice, steady pace. I fell in behind him and quietly we ran about six miles. When he slowed down, I moved beside him and he said something that shook me to my core: "Are we going the right way?"

"Going the right way?!" I shouted. "You don't know?"

He told me he hadn't seen a marker or sign and thought maybe we missed a turn. After some backtracking, we saw a marker and, yes, we indeed had run three to four miles off course. I got angry. I hadn't signed up for a 54-mile race.

After running a few miles, I quit blaming the young runner and blamed myself. In order to run such a race, looking for trail markers and being prepared was my responsibility. Once I owned the situation, I shook off what had happened and dug deep. Putting one foot in front of the other, I began to run my race as planned, not caring about the mile marker, but focused on taking the next step.

This is the nitty-gritty. No one to blame, no playing the victim card, just you and true grit! You must shift into an extra gear of persistence to keep going, depending on yourself and no one else. Though you're not as talented or gifted as others, you have heart. That's more than enough.

Never stop and never quit. This is LifeAbundant365.

Are you doing what you really want to do? Too many of us have settled for a job and not a dream. Somewhere we lowered our standards and accepted less.

Remember, it's all about you! It's all your fault. It's all your choice!

You are designed to be creative. You were built in the image of the creator of all things. If you can reset your mind, undo the lowering of your standards, and control your time, the possibilities for what you might create are unlimited. You control you! You control your attitude and your effort.

We are always seeking to discover new keys to success. Well, there's one characteristic that remains a significant predictor of success: heart!

In this life, we are either in a challenge, coming out of a challenge, or getting ready for the next challenge. This holds true from now until death. What happens to you isn't what matters. How you respond to what happens to you is the difference maker.

Regardless of who you are, or where you come from, achieving greatness is determined by those who decide to achieve greatness. We've always known that the race doesn't always goes to the fastest or the most athletic or smartest person. Sometimes it goes to the one with the most heart or as some say, grit. Grit is the result of endurance and perseverance. Having a never-give-up attitude that comes from the heart, and not the mind.

DIG DEEP:

Have you settled in your life? Why? What happened to the dreams and passion you once had? It's never too late to follow your heart. You just have to decide to move forward and then do it. What's the next step to start you on the path to your dream? Just take the next step. Accept no excuses and focus your energy on moving in the right direction one step at a time. Why not you?

CHAPTER TEN:
Life by Design

THE ONLY DIFFERENCE between the achievers and everyone else is how they respond to obstacles.

How you respond to the daily events you encounter determines your outcomes. This is the secret to a successful life.

You have to believe in yourself because you'll only accomplish what you believe you can. If you don't believe in yourself, nobody else will.

The size of your success is determined by the size of your belief.

Anybody who is the best in any field or endeavor believes they're the best long before they actually prove it. Results follow your beliefs; it's not the other way around. Your life will move in the direction your thoughts take you. You'll never achieve more than you believe you can.

Actions:

- Embrace challenges in your life. Challenges always come our way. Don't run from them and don't ignore them. Failing to address those challenges will only make dealing with those challenges more difficult. Many of our decisions are based on our feelings, which can be problematic because we don't usually feel like doing the things we need to do, or what we know is best for us. Who feels like working out, going on a diet, cutting out sugar, saying "I'm sorry," and so on? In order to go from mediocrity to excellence, we must force ourselves to take the next step. You won't feel like it, so you will have to force yourself to do so until you've formed a habit.

- Do what you already know. Base decisions on knowledge, experience, and gut—not on feelings. We already know what to do: Exercise–Eat Right–Face Problems–Save Money–Help Others–Read Books–Keep Learning. How much different would our lives be if we just consistently did what we already know we should do?

- Taking baby steps to major moves. We should think and dream big, but not to the point where we become overwhelmed by the Big Think. Big dreams can paralyze us, preventing us from moving forward.

- Think big, act small! When I served as a marathon coach for the Nashville Country Music Marathon, I teamed up with "Team in Training" to coach the runners and help them not only finish the race, but raise money for the Leukemia Society. We never mentioned 26.2 miles during our training sessions. I didn't want the runners to have a bumper sticker of 26.2 on their cars. I just didn't want them to even think about the daunting length of the race during their training. My race plan was simple: "One foot in front of the other until we cross the finish line." I would ask my runners things like, "Can you run to the next corner?" "Can you keep going to that mailbox?" "Could you just keep going to the white truck?" One time the white truck started up and pulled off! I just wanted them to use mind over matter to cover a simple distance. Sometimes five miles is a deal killer, but five more minutes is doable.

> My race plan was simple: "One foot in front
> of the other until we cross the finish line."

When you think your tank is empty you usually have enough for a little bit more. That extra effort is the difference between ordinary and extraordinary.

To live a LifeAbundant365 just do the next thing and then the next thing. Just put one foot in front of the other till you cross the finish line.

DIG DEEP:

Are your current beliefs serving you well? If they aren't, change. People once believed the earth was flat. Many of us live by, "I'll believe it when I see it." I say, "Believe it and you'll see it!" Where in your life do you need to interrupt the pattern and change some beliefs? Believe that you too can live a LifeAbundant365!

CHAPTER ELEVEN:
Seek Wisdom

Ask and it will be given to you; seek and you will find; knock
and the door will be opened to you. —Matthew 7:7

DURING YOUR MORNING ROUTINE, seek wisdom.

We give up and give in because our reality doesn't match our expectations.

When was the last time you sought wisdom?

Life is not linear. Life is messy, unpredictable, and chaotic. Expect choppy waters. Don't let that capsize your boat.

Examining the most successful, impactful, and innovative companies, and people, I noticed they all had experienced a life-altering pivot outside their original direction before they found success.

You may already know about Twitter's amazing transformation from Odeo, a podcast subscription network, to the social media monster it is today. The growth of iTunes rendered Odeo obsolete. That led Odeo to come up with the pivots of a micro-blogging, status-updating platform and the subsequent pivots that we now know as Twitter. Today, Twitter is estimated to be valued at more than $10 billion. All thanks to the pivots.

Starbucks wasn't always the behemoth we know today. Even our favorite little coffee shop had to reinvent itself. Starbucks was founded in Seattle in 1971. They began by selling coffee beans and espresso makers. Howard Schultz, now Starbucks' chairman emeritus, loved the coffee, prompting him to transform the company to where everyone could readily taste European-style coffee. If not for his ideas and the company's pivot, you most likely would have to travel to Seattle for your Starbucks fix rather than one of their current 30,000-plus locations around the world.

No one wakes up and declares: I want to feel stuck. I want to feel overweight. I want to feel disconnected. I want to feel sluggish. I want to feel stressed about money.

Still, when we look around, we see stark reminders of our current reality. It's not fun. It's a wake-up call about what we haven't done, how time is passing us by, and how far away we are from where we want to be. However, instead of starting today, we wait. We sit on the sidelines, watching life pass us by.

We will experience challenges, adversity, and chaos at least once every single day.

Pivot points turn good ideas into great ones. Recognizing when to pivot is the key to success. Some never make the pivot. Others see the vision and push through the noise and fear to grasp their dreams. What about you? Where do you need a pivot? What if I moved the needle forward in every area of my life—every single day? What would my life look like in one year?

DIG DEEP:

Where in your life are you operating at Level 10? And where in your life do you need a boost to get above Level 5? Start here! Seek wisdom by reading books, finding a mentor, and imitating someone successful in this arena. Quit your bad habits. What is the plan to make small improvements over a long period of time? Living a LifeAbundant365 is possible by making small adjustments a little at a time. You can do it.

CHAPTER TWELVE:
Digital Dementia

WE ARE THE MOST DISTRACTED GENERATION in the history of the world.

Lack of focus is a major obstacle that separates people from achieving their dreams. In a super-sized, caffeinated, smartphone world, this is obvious. Recent studies show we're now spending an average of ten hours and thirty-nine minutes in front of some type of screen every day.

I now control the first and last hour of the day by eliminating all emails, smart devices, and social media.

If there are more than two people in line at the grocery store, you have no option but to start texting or checking last night's sports scores. Whether this is a matter of social awkwardness, impatience, or the constant need of a digital intravenous drip, we're addicted.

During a flight from Nashville to Miami, Florida, I lost my smartphone. I searched frantically for the device and found nothing. I tried to think: What is the name or number of the car service picking me up? *I don't know, it's in my phone.* And the number for my contact for the event? *In my phone.* I couldn't recall any of the information I needed to make contact with someone from the venue. Digital dementia!

Our device holds all of our information, contacts, and schedule and notes. We no longer memorize numbers, names, appointments, addresses, etc. We are technology dependent.

Are you using technology
or is technology using you?

I used to memorize phone numbers, addresses, dates, birthdays, and other things that now are all on my device. If something happens to that device, like it did to me, we are lost.

Our minds will use any excuse to avoid deep work, but if you harness that tendency, you'll blow the lid open on what's possible for you to accomplish.

DIG DEEP:

Are you using technology or is technology using you? Where did you lose the personal touch to the point that you now connect by text, social media, or email? You rarely communicate in person? How many hours per day are you in front of a screen? To live a LifeAbundant365 we need more personal time and less technology to strengthen our relationships with family and friends. Evaluate your screen time versus your in-person time and adjust accordingly.

CHAPTER THIRTEEN:
The Power of Positive

HOW MUCH WOULD YOU BE WILLING to pay to travel back in time to redo a season of your life?

Why not get it right now? You are in control. It's all about choices.

Become powerfully present! The act of being present rather than preoccupied with the past or the future can have a massive impact on your happiness.

Whatever you create in your life, you must first create in your thoughts. Your life gets bigger or smaller depending on your effort and your attitude. You choose!

Today we worry about this and that, which prevents us from focusing on the now. At times, the worry blocks positive action from taking place. Failure to take positive action is the top reason for us to not reach our potential—more than lack of education, experience, or opportunity.

The problem is living on the surface. Too many of us are a mile wide, but only an inch deep! We have too many things on our plate, so we are spread too thin and can't develop roots.

> The thief comes only to steal and kill and destroy.
> I came that they may have life and have it abundantly.
> —John 10:10

Find that positive mindset and focus on what's important. To have a LifeAbundant365, we need to take action now!

DIG DEEP:

While you're at work, do you find yourself thinking about home? Conversely, when you're at home, do you find yourself thinking about work? We are always traveling in our minds. Learn to become powerfully present and focus on where you are right now! Living a LifeAbundant365 requires your attention and focus. Enjoy the beauty of now!

CHAPTER FOURTEEN:
Move Over … You're in Your Own Way!

Listen to advice and accept discipline, and at the end you
will be counted among the wise. —Proverbs 19:20

OKAY, I GET IT. I can be my own worst enemy. How can I get out of my own way?

Best answer: Stop doing stupid stuff!

Well, that's all I got. Thank you, right? We all do stupid stuff. The lesson is to not repeat the stupid stuff over and over again.

Your current life condition is your fault. What you did, or didn't do, made this reality. How many of you are 100 percent satisfied with every aspect of your life? I'm guessing there aren't a lot of arms in the air.

Distractions are the primary reason for us getting in our own way. We have too many distractions at our fingertips, a list that includes technology, email, devices, and entertainment.

The second way we get in our own way is by saying yes too often. We are doing so many things right, but our constant "yes" to every invitation reduces our effectiveness. To get out of our own way we must start answering "no" more often, and pay attention to what's important.

- Health: Life is short. We are rushing our lives by doing stupid stuff. We lie to ourselves. Small simple easy steps would improve our health. Eat less, and move more! Approximately 90 percent of bad health can be attributed to lifestyle. The law of accumulation will work for or against you. A Hershey Bar a day …

- Family: Today's parents don't discipline or teach their children. Growing up in a house with four children, I often heard, "Turn off that music/TV and do your homework." Today it sounds more like, "Turn down that music/game, I'm trying to do your homework!" Get more involved. What are your plans and goals for your family? What actions are you taking to grow your family? Where does your family need direction and help?

- Finances: Bills are inconvenient yet many of our money problems are self-inflicted. We must take control of our money. Spending all of our money is stupid! Save some of your money, then save some more. When you have a big reserve, there aren't many emergencies. Again, the law of accumulation will work for or against you.

- Business: Service is at an all-time low and we are living in an experience economy. Service has diminished everywhere you go, and it's getting worse. Why? Because the consumer accepts it. Maybe that's because they don't provide exceptional service themselves.

- Faith: Peace, confidence, and comfort come when I put my faith in God. Many things are impossible with man. All things are possible with God. Faith is having a close relationship with God. What a privilege.

People aren't prepared. Most of us are running on autopilot trying to get through the day and not getting something from the day! We excel at consumption, not accomplishment.

We are the only creation that chooses to stop growing. Trees continue to grow until they die. Every other creature continues to grow until death, except us humans!

DIG DEEP:

Where in your life do you need to stop doing stupid stuff? If you start a conversation with "watch this," what's next is probably stupid. And where do you need to say no to time-wasting, energy-sucking people or activities so you can begin to invest in yourself? You are your best shot at success. Living a LifeAbundant365 begins when you do.

CHAPTER FIFTEEN:
Our Beliefs Direct Our Paths

BEFORE 1954 NOBODY BELIEVED A RUNNER could break the four-minute mile.

Roger Bannister changed that belief on May 6, 1954, when he became the first to break the seemingly unbreakable barrier with a 3:59.4 mile. Since Bannister's feat, some 20,000 people have broken the once-thought-impossible barrier, including high school kids.

What changed? That's an easy one. Since the "can't do" part of the equation had been eliminated, the runners knew they too could run a mile in under four minutes.

Where are you going with your life? You thought you would be further along by now. You thought that the early-life problems that plagued you would be gone. But you made some bad choices, a few mistakes, and poor decisions. Now you believe that this is all you will be able to accomplish.

You never believed this could happen to you. Such failure wasn't in your plan. Now you believe it's too late for you. You have to settle!

We become what we think about the most.

Today, many people react instead of taking time to think. They are running on autopilot and past experiences. Comfortable routines serve as their default. They will do anything to not have to think.

To see a permanent change on the outside, you must first create the change of belief on the inside. Your life always moves in the direction of your beliefs. What you believe matters.

You need to believe that you really "can" do all things through "Him" who strengthens you.

When you know who you are, you know who you are not. Be true to yourself.

DIG DEEP:

Do you have places in your life where you simply react versus think? Have you lost the art of thinking for yourself? When was the last time you sat quietly in a room with just you, a legal pad, and pen, and wrote down every thought that came to your mind? Allow yourself the time to think about your life and your future. Where do you want your life to go? If you can think it, you can achieve it! Don't just think it—ink it!

CHAPTER SIXTEEN:
Building Bulletproof Confidence

Therefore, do not worry about tomorrow, for tomorrow will worry about itself. Each day has enough trouble of its own. — *Matthew 6:34*

CONFIDENCE IS NOT SOMETHING YOU HAVE, it's something you create.

Self-esteem issues plague 75 percent of the people in our country. Either they have too high of an opinion of themselves, or too low.

Confidence is not a personality trait, it's a skill. (Introverts can have great confidence and extroverts can have low self-confidence.)

Confidence is the ability to move from thought to action. Being confident doesn't mean you're not scared. Confidence is being scared, but moving forward anyway.

Steve Jobs was asked what he looked for the most when promoting someone to an executive-level position. He answered: "Self-confidence."

Confidence is the belief that you can do all things. It's a skill! One you can train for to gain.

Remember, I can do all things ... Tell yourself this throughout the day, it's true. Your life will be different in the future when you believe this.

Building massive confidence requires the following:

- Trying vs. training. There is a difference. Imagine having severe stomach pain and having to make a trip to the hospital emergency room, where you are seen by two physicians. One tells you he doesn't know for sure what is wrong; however, if he performs surgery, he'll figure it out. He says he will try his best to help you. The second physician comes in with a model of a stomach and identifies exactly where and what your problem is and shows you on the model. He goes on to assure you he is the foremost authority on this specific problem and has done hundreds of these surgeries without any failures. He has trained for years to master this and now trains others. Which one are you going to choose? The one trained, of course.

- The easiest way to build self-confidence is Repetition-Repetition-Repetition. Works every time. Problem is that we quit something before we master it. Practice develops confidence. You have to put in the reps. When Tiger Woods misses a shot in a tournament, he returns to the spot of the miss, or a similar spot, and takes countless practice shots. How would his confidence level be next time he has a similar shot? Repetition is the mother of learning.

- Positive self-talk helps build confidence. Thoughts influence our actions. Muhammad Ali always said, "I am the greatest!"

- Who ya' hanging with? Stop hanging with chickens and start soaring with eagles. Brian Tracey says, "Your income will be the average of the five people you hang around the most." We become a product of our environment, so start hanging around confident people.

> Confidence is not something that you have,
> it's something you create.

- Remove self-doubt (competency builds confidence). Stop listening to self-doubt. If you have to doubt something about yourself, doubt your self-imposed limits. Your potential is unlimited. Believe that. Eliminate the "what if" or "I can't" statements. Control your thoughts!
- Create momentum: Celebrate small wins. Acknowledge your progress.

DIG DEEP:

Where in your life are you lacking confidence? Start there. Stand tall and walk with purpose. Look others in their eyes. Introduce yourself. Above all, practice and put in the reps. Your self-confidence will grow and result in LifeAbundant365!

CHAPTER SEVENTEEN:
The Power of Consistency

"It's not what we do once in a while that shapes our lives.
It's what we do consistently." —Tony Robbins

CONSISTENCY IS DEFINED as the effort to do the things you don't want to do daily in order to succeed and reach your goals and dreams.

Small steps repeated with consistency over time lead to major accomplishments—one foot in front of the other.

Lack of consistency is a weakness shared by all people performing on an average level. When you decide to be better than you were yesterday and take action consistently, you are going to improve. Noah needed a hundred years to build the ark. And I get impatient if a red light takes too long!

Noah's example is a testament to what can be accomplished when a person invests time consistently. Everybody gets the same amount of time every day—1,440 minutes. Even the best plans will fail without the discipline of consistency.

"Success is neither magical nor mysterious. Success is the natural
consequence of consistently applying basic fundamentals." —Jim Rohn

If I agree to do something, I do it. If I schedule a meeting I'm there and on time. Consistency is a game-changer for most of us.

DIG DEEP:

Think about the areas of your current life conditions that could use some consistency. In what areas have you been inconsistent and why? What changes must you make today to begin a life of consistency? Once you are consistent in your actions, your life will become abundant! Decide what's the next step and do it!

CHAPTER EIGHTEEN:
Write Your Own Story

LET'S FOCUS ON THE FORMULA for LifeAbundant365 and success.

What qualifies me to know anything about this?

- I have read over 1,400 books.
- I have attended hundreds of programs and seminars.
- I have completed sixty birthdays of life experience.

My childhood dreams were so exciting and big that I could barely wait to grow up so I could pursue them. I wanted to be a policeman, join the Air Force, become a professional athlete. At one point, I even wanted to become a superhero. One of my best dreams at eight and nine years old was to play for the Cincinnati Reds.

My dad worked for Penn Central Railway as a yard conductor and he drove a charter bus part-time to the Reds games at Crosley Field. He would let me ride the bus to the stadium and watch the games under the following stipulation: "After school, if you can make it to the bus stop on time, you can go to the game."

This started my running addiction. I would watch the classroom clock tick, like waiting to hear a starter's pistol for a race. Once the bell rang, I bolted. Most of the time I made it, though sometimes I did not. Dad wouldn't wait. He rolled on time (win or lose, no participation trophy).

I remember a few times being only steps late and I missed the bus. Talk about a heartbreaker.

Amazingly, once at the ballpark, Dad would turn me loose—alone!

I had the run of the place, seeing all of the '70s "Big Red Machine" teams. I got to know some of the players. Tony Perez, Johnny Bench, Lee Carroll, and Pete Rose would let me on the field, sign anything, then lift me back over the dugout to roam the friendly confines of the ballpark.

I can still hear Dad telling me: "Boy, at the seventh-inning stretch, you head back to the bus." For the most part, I always managed to do so.

Such dreams find us for a reason—our true potential casts a vision of what is possible for us. Through my experience, I could envision playing baseball for the Reds when I grew up.

Dad passed away a few years ago and I found myself as the executor of his estate back in Cincinnati. One evening I attended a Reds game, which proved to be a bittersweet experience. Crosley Field and Riverfront Stadium were both long gone, the players were different, security was tight, and Dad wasn't waiting for me in the parking lot. Memories of sweet dreams past flooded my mind. I hadn't thought about those days for so long. During the weeks following my trip, I replayed those dreams over and over.

Somewhere along the way, we lose that childlike wonder. We trade in our dreams for a job and a mortgage and settle in for the path to an average, common life. Amid the trials and tribulations of life you either forgot your goals, got distracted, or started to believe others who had already lost their dream. They convinced you that yours wasn't possible either.

It doesn't have to be that way. We can still dream and chase our passion—you're never too old to do so! My dream of writing books and becoming a professional speaker came true at fifty-five years old. Now, at age sixty, I'm living my dreams. You can do the same. Just take the next step. That's LifeAbundant365.

To know what to do next we must know what we want. Our inside story. Inside each of us, we have an identity. In order for us to be happy that identity must match our current life conditions. Our reality must match our expectations.

Two words that help us lead our LifeAbundant365:

- Grow. When we are growing, we feel successful and fulfilled.
- Give. Generosity makes us feel complete and productive.

What is your current inner story? What defines your success and abundance? What are your dreams? What does it take for you to feel really successful? What satisfies you most about your current life condition? Why?

The area you are most happy about in your current life condition is such because it matches your expectations, your blueprint. The formula or blueprint for happiness is when life conditions match expectations. That's LifeAbundant365!

What are you unhappy with in your current life conditions? Why?

If your current life condition doesn't match your expectations, you will feel unhappy, disappointed, and discouraged.

We all have a "should be" story inside of us. What we should be is inside everyone. When our life conditions do not match our inner story, we have three options:

- Blame or play the victim. This is really not an option because blaming is not the answer. Blame will not get us to LifeAbundant365 position.

- Change our life condition. Work harder, make additional effort, rethink our action plan, and continue to grind harder.
- Rewrite our story. You are the author of your story. In order for your life to change, you have to change. Small changes done consistently over time lead to major achievements in our life conditions.

DIG DEEP:

Where in your life do you need a change? What would a change mean for you in the future? What will it take to change? What's the next step? Then do it. This time next year you will be happy with your decision and action to advance. You deserve to live out your dreams and you deserve to live LifeAbundant365!

CHAPTER NINETEEN:
Pivot Point

A "PIVOT POINT" is a time in your life when you made a specific decision that caused you to go a different direction.

Pivot points are significant because they delivered you to where you are now, good or bad. Think back over the years to when you made significant changes in your life. Had you made a different decision you would be in a totally different life condition today.

Well, the past is the past. You can't undo what's done. So why are we even discussing pivot points?

Because if you are reading this book, you are alive and capable of making pivotal decisions today and every day. We can change, even if we are heading in the wrong direction. It's that simple. If you find yourself in a hole, stop digging!

The same is true with your current life condition.

No one can change their past, but everyone can pivot and change their future by heading in the right direction. Improving your self-awareness is the best way to recognize pivot points when they cross your path. Being self-aware makes us sensitive to these unexpected and uninvited pivots. Pivot points have made themselves available to you throughout your life, and they will continue to do so. Unfortunately, we are often too busy—or running on autopilot—to take advantage of them. Thus, we stay the course paved with comfort and mediocrity until we think it's too late for us and we settle for average, never looking for the next pivot point.

The decisions and choices we make define us far greater than the circumstances and challenges that impact our lives.

The more self-aware we are and the more open to believing we can do all things, the more chances we will have to choose future pivot points.

Pivot points are happening for us. Not to us.

DIG DEEP:

Put your life on pause for a few minutes. Think about the pivot points you have experienced, and the ones you didn't take. Ask yourself, "What do I really want the rest of my life to look like?" Follow that question with, "What must happen first before it can become a reality?" Then take the first step. Otherwise, you'll never take the second. Action and self-awareness will make you vigilant about accepting future pivot points when they present themselves. You are on your way to a LifeAbundant365!

CHAPTER TWENTY:

Procrastination Always Makes Easy Things Hard and Hard Things Harder

"What's easy to do is also easy not to do!" —Jim Rohn

IF YOU ARE REALLY WORKING—all in on your No. 1 priority right now—then carry on. However, if you are putting off something important to get busy with something less important—stop! You are not using your time wisely.

The fast lane to procrastination is waiting for the "perfect" time. The perfect time is now! Start with where you are and what you have—now!

When I speak about procrastination I always ask my groups two questions:

Question 1: What's the one area of your life that needs to be changed the most?

Question 2: Why haven't you done something more about it?

Normally, we procrastinate because we want to avoid pain or we choose to enjoy pleasure. Fear produces our top pain. You can't wait until you're not afraid anymore (that may never happen) or until you've eliminated all risk (ditto). It will be way too late by then. Be brave, start small, just do something. Do it now. Face your fear. There is no perfect time. The perfect time is now!

We keep waiting for the next great thing to happen in the near future. We're hoping, and believing, that the next great thing that happens will be the key to our happiness. But life continues to be a series of "right now" actions and moments.

Knowing what we want in life makes us more willing to expend energy to achieve it. Not knowing what we really want can be difficult to identify. Many successful professionals are satisfied with their current life conditions, but they still don't know what they really want. Consequently, they continue down the same path unfulfilled and unsatisfied.

What's the solution? Easy. Do what you already know to do. This can be powerfully impactful in our future life conditions. We have so much knowledge about what we should do. Our problem is that we don't take action.

Knowledge without action results in no change. Just knowing you need to do it, but not taking the first step nets nothing. Knowledge doesn't change you—action does!

You don't receive the benefit of knowledge until you act on it!

The power is in the execution! Timing is everything and the time is now! Just take the next step.

DIG DEEP:

Identify one area in your life that needs improvement. It can be something you've known needed changing for a long time, but for some reason you have put it off. Next, define what is the first step you need to take to begin the process of change? Then simply take the next step. Just take one step at a time. One step leads to another, then another, until you cross the finish line. The total change may take some time. However, the change from procrastination to action can change today. Just do it and enjoy a LifeAbundant365!

CHAPTER TWENTY-ONE:
Rules to Live By

I WOULD LIKE TO SHARE the "25 Rules to Live By" that I have learned over the course of my life. Many are self-explanatory, while others require a little explanation to be effective. There are certainly more rules, but these are my Top 25:

1. Jesus is Lord: This is something I've learned and don't doubt. It's about a relationship, not religion. He is first in my life.

2. In a negotiation, never make the first offer: After 4,000 real estate transactions, I've discovered that in negotiations let them start the process by making the first offer. This puts you in the best position.

3. When shaking hands, grip firmly and look them in the eye: Just do it!

4. Hold your heroes to a higher standard and don't compromise: After all they are your heroes—they should act like it.

5. Never shake a man's hand sitting down: This may seem old school, but it shows respect on your part and you'll receive respect from others because of it. This goes for standing when introduced to someone.

6. Don't let a wishbone grow where a backbone should be: When you know who you are, you know who you "are not"! Stand up for what you believe. When you're in a "nonnegotiable" situation, don't back down. Follow your dreams and passion. Don't let others reroute you.

7. Think of others before yourself: Just do it!

8. You get what you give: Give generously. You reap what you sow. Giving starts the getting. I don't know how it works— it just does. Give of your time, talent, and treasure.

9. Write your own eulogy and never stop revising: What do you want people to say about you after you're gone? How do you want to be remembered? You can start now and write your story.

10. Act like you've been there before, especially in a win: Just do it!

11. When entrusted with a secret, keep it: Trust is hard to earn, and even harder to earn back. Just do it!

12. In all critical situations make like a duck: Remain calm on the surface and paddle like crazy underneath.

13. Build relationships every day: At the end of life, we will all agree it is about relationships. Work on them every day.

14. Work harder on yourself than anything else in your life: I didn't learn this 100 percent until later in life. Now I know you can't give away something you don't have. Learn and train every week. Read more books, gain knowledge through videos and podcasts. Once you have knowledge, take action and share.

15. Never turn down a breath mint.

16. Have coffee with a new person every week: The only agenda is building better relationships. I try to have three coffee meetings every week. My objective is to get to know people better. This is life changing.

17. Honor your parents regardless: I understand that not everyone had a storybook childhood with the perfect family—me either. Still, I believe you must honor your parents. I'm not asking you to line up for disappointment or abuse, just forgiveness and honor. Their DNA created the unique person known as you! You are special, creative, and successful from the day you were conceived. Honor your mother and father. You win.

18. Give credit, take the blame: Stop playing the victim card (blaming others) and stop following the "herd mentality." You're bigger than that. Pass credit around generously. Amazingly, credit will find its way back to you. Humble is the word you're looking for.

19. Always protect your family and teammates: I think most of us agree we would lay down our lives for our family. Being a retired U.S. Air Force Warrior, I learned the importance of trusted friends and teammates. I would have made the ultimate sacrifice for them and they would have done the same for me. At a minimum, we need to protect, help, and always be truthful with them.

20. Be confident and humble at the same time: This requires training, not just trying. You have to come to a place in your life where you are sincerely humble and confident. Life will improve in every capacity when you do.

21. Write down your dreams/goals: You improve your success rate of achieving goals markedly when you write them down. Writing down goals gets you nearly halfway there. Enough said.

22. When in doubt just take the next step: Knowing the entire path can be overwhelming and freeze us in place. All of us can take the next step. This builds confidence and momentum in our life. Just do it!

23. Save money: Yes, I'm serious. Doesn't matter how much money you make, save some! Opportunities abound when you aren't in debt.

24. The best deal you can get is the one you can walk away from: Never get in a position where your desires exceed your need in negotiation. You lose your leverage. Do what you must to get the best deal. Patience is required.

25. Make sure everyone you love knows it: Relationships are a top priority. People need to know you love them so tell them, and tell them often.

DIG DEEP:

Read the list and allow it to percolate in your mind. Decide on which rule requires the most attention in your current life conditions, then put in the reps and train to apply that one rule to your life. Master this rule and then attack the next priority. You will see your life conditions improve and live a LifeAbundant365!

CHAPTER TWENTY-TWO:
What Were You Thinking?

THE PROBLEM TODAY isn't what were we thinking, it's have we stopped thinking altogether.

Many of us are running on autopilot mode, which diminishes our ability to think. We merely react and, in many cases, it's a knee-jerk reaction at best. Our lives feel like we're driving on a bumpy road. First, we react this way and then that way. We react, but rarely respond.

Several years ago, I bought a new Infinity Q-45 car that came in a unique green color that I found beautiful. I had never owned a green car, or even seen many green cars. Driving home from the dealership, what color car do you think I saw the most? Green! Suddenly, every other car or truck seemed to be green. Why? Because I sent a clear message to my mind that the color green in vehicles was important, so my brain identified to me every green vehicle around. What happened to me happens to everybody all of the time; we just don't realize it.

Situational awareness requires us to think and be concerned while artificial intelligence is keeping us from having to think for ourselves anymore. We must regain our ability to think. We must cut out the distractions and turn down the noise to allow us to think the old-fashioned way. We must use our memories and brains to figure out our next response.

Situational awareness requires us to think and be concerned while artificial intelligence is keeping us from having to think for ourselves anymore.

Ever turn down the radio while driving and looking for a specific address? This is an example of distraction-free concentration. Sounds from the radio have little to do with preventing us from finding the address, but this mentally allows us to become powerfully present and to focus.

If I organize my life in such a way that I get a lot of long, consecutive, uninterrupted time-chunks (thinking), I can get more of the things that "move the needle" accomplished than when I am just in reaction mode.

Performance always improves once your attention becomes less fractured.

DIG DEEP:

Where in your life do you need a technology intervention? Try an experiment by going without your smart device at the next meal you have with family and friends. Just leave it elsewhere for a few hours, or turn it off. You will be forced to become powerfully present and to interact with your table. Next, break the habit of looking at your phone the first thing in the morning or the last thing at night. Your goal is to control the first hour of your day and the last hour of your night. Go "airplane mode." Use this time to think out loud and to write down your thoughts. Watch your life improve to a LifeAbundant365.

CHAPTER TWENTY-THREE:

Incentives — What Drives You?

AT A SPEAKING ENGAGEMENT for a Mastermind group, I got introduced to one of the members.

"How are you doing?" I asked.

He smirked. "Living the dream."

"Really?" I asked.

"Absolutely not."

"Why not?" I followed, with excitement in my voice.

Why are we not living the dream? And why do we say we are when we aren't?

One of the segments I love the most when I do corporate retreats is asking the group: "What do you really want in life and why?"

Then I observe a bunch of highly educated and successful people struggle to get something on paper. I push hard for them to tell me more by asking the following questions:

- If you could do anything you wanted tomorrow, what would that be?
- What are you most passionate about?
- If you can only do one thing tomorrow, what would that be?

We have to start thinking and dreaming again. Everybody's life has a purpose and many aren't living it. Why not you?

If you were living the dream, what would it mean to you and those you love? How would it change your life conditions? What benefits would you expect if you were indeed living the dream? What would it take to get started on this dream? What's the first step? Are you willing to start, and why?

A willingness to start living with purpose, and knowing the why, is all that's needed to get started. Nothing more. Just stepping out in faith instead of drifting along in mediocrity.

I'm not asking you to quit your current position and wing it. I'm simply asking you to define your purpose/dream and the first step.

When I was writing my first book, *The Surge Effect*, I spoke to an editor who asked me how long I had been writing the manuscript? I told him I'd worked eight or nine years and still had not finished.

Why?

I told him I didn't have the "time."

He said, "Do you go on vacations, do you go out and eat, do you watch television, listen to music, and sleep?"

"Well, of course, I do all of those things!"

Then came his life-changing question. "What are you doing tonight between 9 and midnight?"

"Sleeping," I said.

"Not tonight," he said. "Tonight, and the next 90 nights, we write your book! Are you serious about writing a book or not?"

I considered his remarks and told him, "I'm in!"

Eighty-eight days later we finished the book.

To actually live the dream, you have to make sacrifices and be held accountable. Thinking and seeing the incentives clearly help you persevere, even when you don't feel like it.

DIG DEEP:

What do you really want? What will it take to achieve what you want? What's the first step? Are you serious about living the dream? What are you willing to sacrifice now in order to live the dream later?

Take the next step. Soon you will not only live the dream but also live a LifeAbundant365! That's incentive.

CHAPTER TWENTY-FOUR:
Momentum

Do not despise these small beginnings, for the Lord rejoices to see the work begin. —Zechariah 4:10

MOMENTUM BEGINS BY CREATING A MAP from where you currently are to where you really want to go, knowing that what got you here won't get you there. Change is required! Action is necessary! Start where you are with what you have. No perfect time exists, there is only now. That makes the perfect time now!

Have you ever noticed how discouraged people tend to get more discouraged? Passionate people tend to get more excited? Happy and successful people tend to grow in happiness and success?

The power of momentum is the force that drives this cycle. Momentum is that forward push that overcomes resistance and gets you started. Momentum starts slow and gradually accelerates, like a locomotive. Momentum encourages you to keep going. Momentum is going from a position of "I want" to a position of "I must" long before you get to a sick-and-tired position of "I quit."

Most want to wait until the perfect time, like "once the kids are older," "when I have more money," or "when I get the right equipment." Most fail to achieve their goals because they never take the first step. Momentum is just getting the ball rolling. Momentum is now! Momentum is what's next.

Momentum flows where your focus goes! Your thoughts have momentum. Momentum can work for you or against you. The mind is powerful. Our thoughts have energy. When we focus on a thought, that energy affects what we say and do in response. Once a thought gets enough of our attention, that thought begins to gather momentum.

Behaviors have momentum. Our mind is where the beliefs that drive our behaviors live. Once our patterns of behavior—or habits—have been established, they directly influence our attitudes, thoughts, actions, and words. Habits have their own powerful momentum until we decide to change them.

What you do is what matters the most—not what you think, say, or plan. Simply thinking or talking about momentum will not benefit you. You must take action first. Then the power of momentum takes over.

"The most effective way to do it, is to do it." —Amelia Earhart

DIG DEEP:

Where do you need some positive momentum in your life? Where are you operating at a low level and you know you need to step it up, but so far you haven't made the effort? This is where momentum can work its magic. Choose the area of need and take action to unleash the power of momentum. Don't look for a bull rush at the beginning, but stay focused and your momentum will gradually pick up speed. With momentum on your side you will be on the right road to living a LifeAbundant365.

CHAPTER TWENTY-FIVE:

The Dream Is Free. The Hustle Is Sold Separately.

"Things may come to those who wait, but only the things left by those who hustle." —Abraham Lincoln

ARE YOU MOVING QUICKLY and with purpose, but not really getting anywhere? Why? What's the answer to break through? New job? Promotion? More education? Luck? I don't believe in luck.

The answer is more hustle!

Many of us are not in the job of our dreams or doing what we believe in. We are simply working to pay off debt, provide for our family, save for retirement, etc. We can't see what's going on around us because we have our nose to the grindstone for forty years, retire, then die. No thanks! Life doesn't have to be that way!

Without hustle, talent will only carry you so far. Hustle opens up your true potential.

When my family was young, I took them to Hilton Head. Every year I would tell my wife, one day we're going to own a beach house. Fast-forward many years and I would tell my wife, "One day I'm going to write a book."

Ten years ago, we bought a beach house. Two years ago, I released my new book. How? Hustle. I didn't have the money, time, education, training, or experience to accomplish the things I have accomplished. What I do have is hustle. And you do, too!

"Contrary to popular opinion, the hustle is not a new dance step—it is an old business procedure." —Fran Lebowitz

Every once in a while, people tell me that hustle can have a negative connotation—like you're a shark hustling someone in a game of pool. I'll stick to the definition that's noble. Hustling is not about cheating, and it's definitely not about a dance move. It's an unstoppable, enthusiastic way of making money and creating a business. Lebowitz's quote reminds us there is nothing new about hustle. Hustlers have been making the world turn for quite some time now. Why should we question their tried-and-true ways?

Hustle means you grind while others play. You consistently outwork everyone else and you do a little extra every day. To hustle you have to sacrifice. You might need to miss a game, a party, or a trip in order to get a few steps closer to your dream. A real hustler is willing to sacrifice who he or she is now to become who he or she wants to be later.

DIG DEEP:

Take a deep inventory of where you want to go and where you currently are. Make a list of what has to be accomplished before you get to where you're going. Write down what you will give up in order to get things done. Then decide what are the first steps to hustling. Maybe you get off work at 5 p.m., go home, have dinner, and see the family until 9 p.m., and then you work on your side hustle from 9 to 11 p.m. Hustling is to sacrifice who you are now to be who you want to be later. That's LifeAbundant365.

CHAPTER TWENTY-SIX:
Elephants Don't Bite ... Mosquitos Do!

HAVE YOU EVER BEEN BITTEN by an elephant? How about a mosquito?

It's the "little" things that get you!

In this chapter we are going to address the "little" things and how your life will change dramatically if you pay attention to those little things.

Stop deceiving yourself! Many of us are our biggest problem. We blame the economy, other people, our company, our family, our friends, our childhood, our lack of support, our poor education, our pitiful training—everyone but ourselves!

I'm reminded of the child who found himself under a coffee table and couldn't get out. He banged his head and got mad at the table and everybody else around him. What he failed to recognize was the fact he was the problem. Being angry and not looking for solutions had used up all of his energy.

We are the same way. When we get into a bind, we blame others, and we don't look for the solution within ourselves, making us the problem and not the solution. Playing the victim card is easy, but doing so places us in a diminished position where we become uncommitted, disengaged, discouraged, disappointed, and alienated from the people who want to help us. The victim card doesn't provide solutions or help.

I read a book a few years ago that discussed the "compound effect"—the principle of reaping huge rewards from a series of small, seemingly insignificant, smart choices repeated over a longer period of time!

What I found most interesting about this process was that even though the end results were massive, the steps in the moment didn't feel significant. They were actually easy, but beware as Jim Rohn said, "What's easy to do is also easy not to do."

Whether you're using this strategy for improving your health, relationships, finances, business, spiritual life, or anything else, the changes are so subtle, they're almost imperceptible.

These small changes offer little or no immediate result, no big win, no obvious I-told-you-so payoff. So why bother?

Most people get tripped up by the simplicity of the compound effect. For example, they quit after the eighth day of running because they're still overweight. Or they stop making contributions to their IRA after a few years because they could use the cash—and it doesn't seem to be adding up too much anyway.

What they don't realize is that these small, seemingly insignificant steps completed consistently over time will create a massive difference.

DIG DEEP:

How many times in the past have you been focused on the next big thing and overlooked the little things in life? Where in your life are you chasing the big deal and not taking the little deals all around you? Start today by investing in yourself consistently, even when it's small and insignificant. The trick is to keep moving (at any pace) to get to your best life ever. Save money and time every day. One day soon you will be living a LifeAbundant365!

CHAPTER TWENTY-SEVEN:

So You Want to Ride the Success Train?

"The two most valuable days in a person's life are the day you were born and the day you find your purpose." —Mark Twain

THE JOURNEY IS MORE FUN if you know where you're going.

People often find achieving success difficult. But if you don't know what success is, how will you ever achieve it? That's why I want to help you identify a definition of success that will work for you. Success is a journey.

You must have a picture of where you are and where you are going. To move forward, we need to have vision, dreams, desires, passion, and purpose.

You must honestly answer these questions:

- Who am I? Not who your boss-spouse-family-friends want you to be, but deep down inside, who are you?
- What's my value? If you don't know how valuable you are, how will you ever know when you become more valuable? You get paid for the value you bring to the marketplace. What is your current value?
- What's my purpose? Why are you here? What's your mission?

- What do I want to do with the rest of my life? Think and dream big. You already know this even if you aren't aware.

You are preparing to go on a lifelong journey—the journey to success—and this trip has the potential of taking you a long way— maybe farther than you've ever imagined or dreamed. To make the trip, you'll need some things: A vision of where you want to go, answers to your questions about success, knowledge of what success is to you, and the ability to change, or let go, and continue growing.

Why are you here? What are your gifts and talents?

"I would rather have it said, 'He lived usefully' than 'He died rich.'"
—*Ben Franklin*

Ben Franklin lived his life accordingly. Instead of seeing success in terms of how much material stuff and money he could make, Franklin focused on how many people he could help. To him, being useful was a huge reward.

Zig Ziglar said, "You will get all you want in life if you help enough other people get what they want."

I want to be remembered as a guy who added value to the lives of others. I've made so many mistakes in my life, I know what not to do for sure. And I've had some great successes in my life, so I know what to do as well. I want to share these truths with others.

I've learned that it's not so much what we take from the world, but how much you put in it. Seeing wealth and status as forms of fulfillment is an illusion and a fleeting experience. To live a life of abundance, I now understand that I don't want my life to be measured by dollars and stuff.

I want to live out a different version of success, a more meaningful one, one where I consistently improve myself and always positively influence other people.

"Work harder on yourself than you do on anything else." —Jim Rohn

Time is perhaps the top pressure faced by mankind. At age sixty, I feel a sense of urgency to make sure my time and energy are invested in working hard on myself daily.

The better questions you can ask yourself, the better answers you'll receive.

DIG DEEP:

Questions like the following really get your brain working overtime:

- Where am I now?
- Where would I like to go?
- How do I get there from here?
- How long will it take?
- What should I pack/unpack for my journey?
- How do I handle the detours?
- Do I travel alone or with somebody?

Taking the time to think and answer these questions will lead you to a successful life in so many areas. Taking action will bring you through a life lived well. Now that is LifeAbundant365!

CHAPTER TWENTY-EIGHT:
Keys to a Great LifeAbundant365

A GREAT LIFE doesn't just happen by accident.

A great life is a derivative of wisely investing your time, energy, thoughts, and hard work toward what you want your life to be in the future. Rather than flying by the seat of your pants and reacting to what comes next, a great life is achieved by using your 1,440 daily minutes in a creative way.

Customize these keys to fit your own needs and lifestyle, and start creating your own LifeAbundant365 today!

Simplify. Keeping it simple is a great formula for LifeAbundant365. Simplifying is not about removing the work from your life, rather it's freeing up time and energy for the work you enjoy and for your purpose. In order to create a great life, you must simplify yours first. What should I pack/unpack for my journey?

Grind. A great life is the result of your best effort. You can't put in minimum effort and expect maximum results. Grinding will create your great life, but you need to make adjustments and sacrifices. That will require changing how you invest your time, or choosing how to spend—or not spend—your money. Looking for new ways to invest your energy that will help align you with your definition of a great and abundant life. Life will reward your best effort with the best results.

Prioritize. How do I handle detours? A LifeAbundant365 is the result of creating priorities and maintaining. Exhausting your days by reacting to the next challenge that gets your attention is a trap. To avoid falling into that trap, you need to focus on intentional thinking and using the time, energy, and money you have in a way that's most important to you. Strive to focus and remove the habits and obstacles that get in the way of you making sure you are honoring your priorities.

Savings. Few emergencies in life arrive when you have money in the bank and time to think. A great life has reserves—reserves of things, time, energy, and money. Having $50,000 in a reserve/savings account when your air conditioner unit goes out turns the $4,500 replacement cost into a nuisance rather than an emergency. Savings are important because they help reduce the fear of consequences. That allows you to make decisions based on what you really want instead of what fear dictates.

Eliminate distractions. We are the most distracted generation in the history of the world. A LifeAbundant365 is the result of eliminating distractions. Up to 75 percent of your mental energy can be tied up in things that are draining and distracting you. These distractions usually involve a screen on a device. You must take control of your day to eliminate distractions from your life. Start with controlling the first and last hours of your day. Next, dedicate ten to fifteen minutes a day to practice thinking and not reacting. Stop worrying about tomorrow and use your energy on today.

The battlefield of your mind. A great life is the result of controlling your thoughts and taking every thought captive. Positive and motivated people have specific written goals and they're always looking for ways to achieve them. You create what you think and believe. What you think about, you bring about. A thought turns into a belief that becomes an action and results in your current life conditions. Watch your self-talk and make sure it is helpful, not negative. Guard your mind.

The power of NOW! Just start! A great LifeAbundant365 is the result of just starting. Start where you are with what you have. Don't wait for a promotion, or until the kids get older, or the weather is better. What you do today will make a difference in your life tomorrow. Every step forward is a step closer your future and your dream. Take the next step!

DIG DEEP:

Customize these "keys" to fit your own needs and lifestyle, and start creating your own LifeAbundant365 today! Each key opens a multitude of opportunity to improve your life conditions.

CHAPTER TWENTY-NINE:
Live a Life of Thanks

WE HAVE MORE TODAY, but enjoy less.

Seemingly, no matter how hard we work or how much money we accumulate, we are not happier. Why? Somewhere along the line we began to believe that we are entitled to more, which has made us discontent.

Fortunately, contentment can be learned and overflow in thanks.

First, we need to focus on the next generation. When I was a kid, my father always told me, "Don't do as I do, do as I say."

Dad drank alcohol and smoked cigars, but he would not tolerate his kids doing either. Things were so different when I grew up. We didn't wear helmets to ride skateboards or bikes. We drank out of a hosepipe. We never had car seats—now kids ride in them until they can drive! I rode in the back window of a '65 Ford while my sisters and brother rode in the seats. One tap of the brakes and I was rolling over them and onto the floor. That was normal. My parents chain-smoked while they drove us to school. I always told them, "If you love your kids you would crack the windows." So many things I learned not by listening, but by watching.

Most of us have heard that "values are caught, not taught."

Simply sharing the truth with our children isn't good enough. We need to walk the truth in front of them. Be an example. Without learning thankfulness, children can grow up to look like the world around them. For those of you who aren't parents, setting a good example for the children in your life should still be a consideration. They watch everything you do and say.

It is good to give thanks to the Lord, and to sing praises to Your name, O Most High; To declare Your lovingkindness in the morning, and Your faithfulness every night. —Psalm 92:1-2

I've noticed during these difficult days in our nation, people are either responding with a deeper gratitude and appreciation for the simple blessings of life or they are lapsing into grumbling and discouragement about how tough things are. One thing remains clear: Giving thanks to the Lord is still good, even in these challenging times of division and political correctness. United we stand and divided we fall. Stand up for your beliefs and give thanks for what's going right. Don't focus on what's gone wrong. Be thankful.

I experienced some difficult years from 2008 through 2012. I found myself immersed in the real estate world of sales, rentals, investment, development, and mortgage and title business. Real estate was all I knew. After a twenty-year career in the U.S. Air Force, I entered the civilian world and discovered the Air Force had been a major part of my identity. And suddenly, I was no longer that person. I'd lost my identity. Real estate became my new identity.

I dove headfirst into the wonderful world of real estate, and my dedication paid off. From 1992 through 2006, I experienced great success and growth. Then the economy tanked and the real estate world followed suit. That rocked my world.

Talk about extremes. I went from riding high and being so happy to the lowest of lows and grumbling daily. I watched my little empire deconstruct piece by piece as the economy continued its downward spiral. That difficult journey turned my life upside down. Suddenly I wasn't happy anymore. My daily struggles led to a life of discouragement and disappointment. Everyone in my life felt the change in me and the corresponding negative vibe I projected.

Finally, I decided to exit the pity-party train of negativity to board the gratitude train.

I began to give daily thanks for my health, family, and salvation, celebrating the smallest of wins of the day. Through that change, I realized it's impossible to be negative and depressed when you are being thankful and grateful. Momentum began to swing my way. Opportunities showed up. Those opportunities were slow at first, then more and more opportunities knocked on my door. I went all in. I claimed the promises of God and began to believe that praising Him and thanking Him for leading me to a happy state.

Fast-forward to today. I'm living my best life ever and my blessings have continued to grow as quickly as my gratefulness. Some of you reading this may see no way out right now. Please understand the following:

Jesus looked at them and said, "With man this is impossible, but with God all things are possible." —Matthew 19:26

You must take the next step. Start moving from where you are this moment to where you want to be. Never quit—never stop!

And whatever you do, in word or deed, do everything in the name of the Lord Jesus, giving thanks to God the Father through Him. —Colossians 3:17

Whether we are working, driving, running, walking, breathing, showering, or whatever, we are told to be thankful.

DIG DEEP:

Are you focused on what is wrong and not thankful for what is right? If you allow your focus to be on the negative, you are putting yourself in a diminished state. Stop. Get off the train to nowhere and jump on the gratitude train. You will have to force yourself to do so throughout the day because you won't always feel like doing so. Sit down immediately and write in your journal five things you are grateful for. Schedule appointments in your day to give thanks for these things. Tell others about how grateful you are for them. Add to your list weekly. Consistency is the secret key to LifeAbundant365!

CHAPTER THIRTY:
The Best Is Yet to Come

SAY IT WITH ME, "It is possible!"

Do you want to be successful?

Do you expect to be successful? Why? What have you done to build that expectation of being successful? Are you fit for the fight this year? That fight will arrive in many different forms such as anger, disappointment, jealousy, envy, sickness, family challenges, money problems—rest assured, a fight is coming.

Do you have a plan for the rest of your life, or are you just playing it out day by day? I have always had another plan for when I finish this season. The U.S. Air Force was a season. The real estate industry brought another season. Becoming an author and launching my speaking career initiated the season I'm currently experiencing.

Each new season is bigger and more satisfying than the one before. I can do all things!

Audience members at my events have often told me, "I could never speak in front of a group" or "I could never write a book" or some other self-limiting belief they have nurtured over a long period. Eventually they come to believe they can't do something because they've convinced themselves they can't. But they can do it, because they can do all things if they would just believe and take action.

Dwelling on your problems won't fix them. In the process, a negative attitude is bred that improves your chances of future failures. Find a positive attitude instead by looking for solutions and improvement. A positive attitude will allow you to find the good, even in the bad, making this year your best year ever!

Most don't have a plan. They complete their education, get a job, get married, have a family, retire, then die—never realizing their dreams. Never living their best life ever! They had dreams and goals. What happened? They got busy, tired, complacent, then settled for less, believing that's all there was for them.

Going with the flow can be good, but being aware of the direction you're headed is also important. I once heard, and now believe, that when you always do what is easy, your life will be hard! When you do what is hard, your life will be easy!

What is your ultimate goal in life? Your dream is still possible! Stop drifting.

When things go wrong, don't go with them!

Do you find yourself feeling frustrated on a weekly basis? Do you feel like a zombie, waking up each day to the same repetitive cycle that seems never-ending? Has the quality of your life diminished over time, resulting in a loss of energy, and enthusiasm for the future? Somewhere you have accepted something and accommodated your life for stuff that was never meant to be.

Nothing "just happens." Everything has a beginning. We all get frustrated from time to time. Life can be overwhelming. Without understanding the direction our lives are headed, and why they're headed there, tough times will seem overwhelming. Life doesn't have to be that way. You can improve the quality of your life by making a few small adjustments to your routines by altering your behavior and your way of thinking and talking. And keep in mind that you're not alone. We all go through periods of frustration, anxiety, fear, upset, and worry.

Your enemy's No. 1 target is the arena of your mind. To fight the enemy, you need to do the following:

- Create your ideal day. If you're constantly struggling to fit everything in, write out how you would like your day to look. The list should include all activities you would like for the day to be considered successful. Prioritize the top tasks you must accomplish this day. Once you do this, the clutter will start to fall away.

- Eliminate distractions. How much of your day is spent being reactive? If you often feel like the day flew by but you didn't make any progress, you might be allowing too many distractions. Allowing yourself to get distracted enables you to get used to being distracted. Sound familiar? Carve out some time each day—no phones, no interruptions from co-workers or family members—to work on the things that are most important to you. I call these things the "Vital Few." These must be mastered and completed to be successful and valuable in the marketplace and life.

- Think of yourself now the way you want to become later. We rise to the level of our expectations. How do you define yourself? When do you decide what you can and can't do? Who established these limiting beliefs?

Get started on your one game-changer goal. You get to set the standard in your life. Raise it! What is your standard? When did you set it?

When I travel to speak to organizations of all sizes, I encourage audience members to pick one goal that is going to be a complete game changer both personally and professionally—the goal that once achieved will completely change the trajectory of their lives. Most people may have goals, but few sit down and take the time to think about their game-changer goal.

DIG DEEP:

There is no pause button on life. Most of us experience a moment where we just need to step back and think and evaluate what's next in our lives. At the same time, we must understand that the world keeps spinning with or without us. We all have challenges and we deal with them in our own way. I'm just saying, don't step back for too long. Recovering and advancing becomes harder the longer you stay off course. Understand and tell yourself you can do all things and define who you want to become and what's the next step to get there. Then do it. The choice is yours, so choose wisely, my friends. LifeAbundant365 is waiting for you right now. Just move forward.

CHAPTER THIRTY-ONE:
Fulfillment

OUR SOCIETY LIVES in a state of discontent.

We're not happy with anything—our political leaders, our spouses, our careers, our families, or the things that we have accumulated. Our houses are too small, our cars are too old, and our computers don't have the latest technology.

What's a person to do to find fulfillment in such a shaken, discontented world?

How would you change if you discovered you had only six months to live? What would you do with the life you had left? What would your priorities be? How would you value time?

I asked myself what I would do if I found that I had just six months to live. What would that six months look like?

We don't know exactly how we would respond to a situation like this until we are in the middle of it. I believe I would first get my business affairs in order. Make sure my family knew about everything I do, like bank accounts, passwords, life insurance information, and such.

I know Jesus as my Lord and Savior, so I would make sure my family and friends accepted Him too. I would spend more time with Jesus as I prepared to meet Him face-to-face.

Next, I would make sure to spend private time with each family member letting them know how much I love them and why. I always try to show family and friends what is most important to me every day. I would remind them again.

I would try to reconcile any strained relationships. I want to forgive those who have trespassed against me and me against them.

Finally, I would become a "world-class repenter." I want to keep a short list of where I have sinned and fallen short as I prepare to receive my reward.

As I made this list of answers, a question continued to pop up in my mind: "Why do I have to wait until I have six months to live? Why not do all these things now?"

Now, you answer the questions to define what is the most valuable to you. And the nice part is, you don't have to wait for a message about the end to ask and answer the questions. Do it now! Go to your journal and begin the much-needed process of deciding for yourself the power of these questions and answers.

All of us crave fulfillment, but few of us know how to attain it. I've learned that those who have lived fulfilled lives, and are continuing to do so, didn't attain that state from a success-money-material gain, rather they found a life of purpose.

Most of the time they have been living their passion and their dream. They looked forward to serving and helping causes bigger than themselves. They give massive effort and they do their best even when they don't feel like doing so.

Have you ever felt neutral, or empty, after completing a personal or professional goal? That happens to many of us. We've been focused for so long on achieving a goal, but when we achieve that goal, we find ourselves thinking, "Is that all there is?" Instead of feeling elated and fulfilled, we feel empty.

A fulfilled life means staying true to you. Words like abundance, courage, contribution, fearless, giving, present, endurance, and consistent describe a fulfilled life. The desire for more money and power is a never-ending journey. Acquiring stuff doesn't contribute to fulfillment.

Neither money nor power is related to greater levels of happiness and fulfillment. Professional and personal successes are important to our sense of fulfillment, but they are just one part of something larger. For me, more money and power aren't the priorities they were when I was younger.

When I retired from the U.S. Air Force and began my season as a business owner and entrepreneur, I found myself buying an upscale home, cars, clothes, and other designer stuff. There is nothing wrong with nice stuff, but fast-forward twenty-something years and I can see clearly that those things that defined achievement or success to me back then did not add to my sense of fulfillment.

Fulfillment is a happy state of mind. Some say it's their happy place—a sense of joy and inner contentment regardless of what's going on outside—like the feeling you get from setting up your tent before the storm.

Fulfillment is a satisfied state of mind. You can control this position with some practice.

> Not that I speak from want, for I have learned to be content in whatever circumstances I am. I know how to get along with humble means, and I also know how to live in prosperity; in any and every circumstance I have learned the secret of being filled and going hungry, both of having abundance and suffering need. I can do all things through Him who strengthens me. —Philippians 4:11-13

Fulfillment is a learned response. We've all known people who have gone through severe challenges, yet they seem successful and content on the outside. I know of warriors who came back from the battlefield with less than they had beforehand, yet they seemed to be happier than ever. Living a fulfilled life is more about choice, persistence, and endurance than it is circumstances.

No pause button exists to prevent the world from spinning around. Life goes on with or without you. You must decide how your future is going to be lived out. Will it be a life of fulfillment or discontent? It's all up to you.

DIG DEEP:

Where in your life are you restless and discontent? Where have you confused achievement with the art of fulfillment? What in life brings you true peace and joy? What do others really need from you more than anything material? Where are you fulfilled in your life right now? Write in your journal the things that matter to you the most.

CHAPTER THIRTY-TWO:
Personal Growth

IF YOU WANT TO GROW, you have to let go!

That means letting go of past rejections, failures, and poor choices. For many of us, that means letting go of control. If we have control issues—and know we have control issues—letting go is not the easiest thing to do. But again, we can't grow if we won't let go.

Inner beliefs and values direct our paths, resulting in our external reality. What you believe is important. Those stories you've told yourself over the years—though some are not true—you now believe. Those beliefs cause you to make decisions, settle and not fight, or forget about your dreams. If your beliefs are not serving you, change them. Remember, once upon a time most people believed the earth was flat.

Make a promise to yourself: "I promise to never play the victim card—ever again!"

Take ownership for your current life condition. Get out of the herd mentality and run your own race.

When I teach "Personal Growth" to the corporate world, I'm fascinated when I observe corporate-level executives realize that they are in a professional and personal rut. The leadership of the company has settled into a routine. Day after day they do the same thing, yet they expect different results. Then we interrupt the pattern and give them a new perspective. We start with some simple changes, then graduate into deeper activities.

Something simple like cross training is a good start. We have an executive manager from one department trade places with a manager from another department for a week (walk a mile in another's shoes). That never fails to shake things up. Everybody begins to gain a better understanding of what others do.

Personal growth is *the* launching pad for LifeAbundant365. Regardless of your age, or season of life, you can still grow. Personal growth never retires or expires. Personal growth requires us to change.

> *Until we all attain to the unity of the faith, and of the knowledge of the Son of God, to a mature man, to the measure of the stature, which belongs to the fullness of Christ. As a result, we are no longer to be children, tossed here and there by waves and carried about by every wind of doctrine, by the trickery of men, by craftiness in deceitful scheming; but speaking the truth in love, we are to grow up in all aspects into Him who is the head, even Christ. —Ephesians 4:13-15*

Growth requires intention, attention, and action. You must seek and search for growth opportunities as if your future depends on it, because it does. Growth doesn't just happen. You must seize it while you can. Every test of endurance is also a test of self-control.

> *"The secret key to personal and professional growth is to work harder on yourself than anything else." —Jim Rohn*

Growth requires intention, attention, and action.

Attitude, vocabulary, self-esteem, and personality are a few areas on which you can immediately begin to work. What you do every day determines your future life condition.

How much time have you allotted every day for personal growth? Could you show me your written plan for personal growth right now? How many hours per day and days per week have you committed to personal growth? What actions/activities do you consistently do to improve and grow you?

You must know the following for the current condition of every area in your life:

- What are your strengths?
- What are your weaknesses?
- Where you are now?
- Where do you want to go? What's the farthest and highest you can imagine going? Think big! Stop straining to see yourself better than you really are. Simply make an honest evaluation of you.

Growth requires change. Change is rarely a matter of ability. More often change comes down to a matter of motivation. Growth is very personal. No one can grow for you.

Don't confuse activity with growth. We live in a society that loves busy. Busy doesn't guarantee success or growth. Busy guarantees we will be tired.

DIG DEEP:

Wishing, waiting, or wanting is the enemy of personal growth. I hear people at my events say "I wish ... " or "I want ... " To which I say: "No you don't or you would have it or do it."

What are a couple of activities you need to start in order to become more valuable and move toward your potential? What are a couple of activities you need to stop in order to grow toward your potential?

Start today with one activity to start and stop to see personal growth. Just start!

CHAPTER THIRTY-THREE:
Don't Get Trapped

"Sometimes I win and sometimes I learn." —John Maxwell

LIFE IS MESSY and full of traps. We need situational awareness or we can be easily ensnared, rendering ourselves ineffective, and putting us out of the game.

The following are a few traps to avoid:

- The Expectation Trap. We start something new—a job, a relationship, a diet or fitness program—only to discover it's more difficult than we thought and not what we expected. Now what? Unfortunately, this is the point where many give up, rationalizing, "I tried everything and it didn't work for me." Why? We overestimate our abilities and underestimate expectations, creating a situation that doesn't line up with our expectations. So, we quit.

- The Change Trap. Change is the only constant where change is concerned. Nothing remains the same, and things will change whether we approve of the change or not. We cannot stop change. The best we can do is to accept it. No matter how bad or good your current life condition is, change will happen. Things are not the same as they used to be. Our interests change. Our friends change. Our lives change. Not all change brings positive growth, but without change there can be no growth at all.

- The Failure Trap. When you won't try something new because you fear failure. If you aren't making mistakes in life, you aren't living, or trying anything new. You never fail until you quit. Don't fall into this trap. Live and learn. Take calculated risks and take chances. How else will you grow? Avoid this trap!

- The Unforgiveness Trap. We've all been treated badly by someone at some time for some reason, so we're always going to have something to be angry or upset about. But what's done is done. The only question is whether we can let it go and forgive. Unfair treatment is inevitable—forgiveness is optional. Unforgiveness will merely add an additional burden to our lives and diminish us. We don't have to line up for additional abuse, just forgive and move on with your life. Don't be trapped by unforgiveness. You'll lose.

- The Timing Trap. Past losses make us hesitate or lament that "right now isn't the right time." In reality, the perfect time is now. Start where you are and with what you have. The key is to start.

- The Not Understanding That We Get What We Give Trap. One of the most consistent realities in the universe is that what you plant now you will harvest later. Seeds produce after their kind. The thoughts and actions we sow now, we will harvest soon. Not everyone who's lazy will fail to have a stable career and financial life—but many will. That should not come as a shock. Not everyone who treats their friends badly will lose their friends—but many will. That should not come as a shock, either. We should believe that what we do today will impact our future. I can't explain why this works, it just does. I don't know how my cell phone works either, but I know it just does.

DIG DEEP:

Think about your current life condition. Do you find yourself stuck in a life trap? Are you about to walk into a life trap? The best defense for avoiding the traps of life is to become aware. Turn off autopilot and turn on your eyes, ears, and mind to recognize the traps before you're stuck. If you are currently stuck, awareness is your key to escaping. First, you must realize the trap that constantly snares you, or holds you back. You can then begin the freeing process of undoing the beliefs and actions that got you there.

If you're in the trap of unforgiveness, forgive. Release that person from your unforgiveness—free them and you will free yourself. Think of all the traps you've encountered in your life—the ones that trapped you and the ones you avoided. Become in tune to both. Know that your beliefs and actions will determine your direction and help you identify the traps ahead. Living a trap-free life brings you LifeAbundant365.

CHAPTER THIRTY-FOUR:
Wash Your Face

YOU NEED TO WASH YOUR FACE every morning and every night. I'm not talking hygiene here, I mean wash from your face yesterday's disappointment, discouragement, anger, or worry.

If I did something wrong when I was a kid, or I was unhappy about something, my mother would say, "It's written all over your face."

My facial expression made my mood or thoughts obvious to Mom. I learned to "wash my face" and start fresh every morning and every night. Nobody wanted to see my dirty face.

In business, clients, management, and co-workers don't need to see your mess from yesterday. And you don't need a constant reminder either. The simple habit of washing your face every morning will give you a fresh start.

We can only control our attitude and our effort. The washing your face habit will improve your attitude and energize your effort. Others will notice your determination and they will help you gain momentum, all because you'll be easier to get along with and to be around. Wash your face!

Washing your face needs to be a daily habit that helps you create energy and the right mindset to tackle the challenges of any day. Washing your face is just the beginning. It will jump-start your day.

The best way to jump-start tomorrow morning is by what you do the night before. Review your plan and priorities for tomorrow. Make changes or updates to your agenda. Lay out the clothes you plan to wear. Turn off your smart device an hour before bedtime. Make notes for tomorrow tonight. Place your smartphone/device in another room from your bed so you won't be on it. You'll have to officially get up instead of hitting the snooze button when the alarm goes off.

Washing your face may sound like a simplistic and ridiculous action for helping to change your life, but try it. The exercise is the start of setting your mind. While you are washing your face you are telling yourself, "Today is a fresh start." You are forgiving and forgetting yesterday and the past. You are giving yourself every opportunity to make the most of your day and to get something out of the day instead of just getting through it.

The habit of washing your face will soon become your favorite part of the day. You are signaling a new day, a fresh start, and a new beginning right there at your sink.

DIG DEEP:

Wash your face the very first thing tomorrow morning. Tell yourself you're going to have a great day. Today is happening for you and not to you. Forgive and forget the problems and disappointments from yesterday. Welcome this fresh start and set your mind on the good things in life. Be grateful for what's going right. Momentum is now on your side and the day is going to get better from here on. Washing your face leads to LifeAbundant365!

CHAPTER THIRTY-FIVE:
Law of Diminishing Intent

"SORRY I MISSED TRAINING LAST WEEK, coach," said one of the athletes I coached for the Country Music Marathon in Nashville. She went on to let me know that she would never miss another day of training and that she would work twice as hard to make up for her absence.

Guess who was absent again after only two days of training. Imagine my surprise. I received another apology and promise from her that she would work harder and not miss another training session. Over the next few weeks I saw less and less of my athlete and less of her apologies and promises.

What happened is defined as "The Law of Diminishing Intent"!

Today I can make all kinds of convincing promises about tomorrow and believe—and fully intend—to keep my promises. Then tomorrow or the next day arrives and I don't feel like following through, or I'm too busy or (fill in the blank excuse). Each day after, my intent will continue to diminish even more. I sincerely felt committed at the time, but that commitment just wasn't as important the next morning and even less important the day after that. Pretty soon I have no intention of following through with my commitment—ever!

Neglect is always the first step toward quitting. Let's say you are excited and committed to get in better physical shape. You enlist friends to join a gym with you, buy some new workout clothes and gear, and some running shoes, then off you go to build the perfect body. For the next two weeks you are humming along. Every morning you're at the gym at five o'clock grinding hard and doing well. Then comes week three and one morning you just don't feel like going to the gym. So, you don't go, but you promise your friends and yourself you'll be a beast the next day. The next day arrives and you are less than beast-mode and leave the workout early. Can you guess what the future holds for your perfect body 2.0?

The Law of Diminishing Intent is in full force all the time and we have to be on guard.

DIG DEEP:

Reflect back when you last experienced the Law of Diminishing Intent. Write down what happened. What regrets do you have now? What could you have done differently? If you could have a "Do Over" what would you change?

The Law of Diminishing Intent will interfere in every area of your life if you don't prepare by defining the following:

- What do you really want to accomplish?
- Why do you want it? (What will achieving it mean to you and those you love?)
- What obstacles and challenges will you encounter along the way?
- What is your plan to overcome the challenges and avoid the Law of Diminishing Intent?
- Practice-Practice-Practice!

By stopping the Law of Diminishing Intent, you are on the path to LifeAbundant365!

CHAPTER THIRTY-SIX:
The Second Wind

Enoch walked with God ... —Genesis 5:24

GETTING IN PACE WITH GOD is painful work, and it's even harder to keep in step with Him because His stride is swift and purposeful and it wears you down, but if you keep going, you get your "second wind."

The second wind is a phenomenon in long-distance running—like a marathon or an ultramarathon—when an exhausted runner who appears unable to continue suddenly finds a renewed strength to continue at top performance with less exertion.

I enjoyed endurance running and races for many years. Learning how to transition from running 10K distance to the half marathon struck me as a natural progression, but not an easy one. Naturally, as my distance grew, my pace slowed. Slower pace meant slower finishes, which didn't set well with me, a young military warrior. I felt compelled to pick up the pace and finish in a better position every race. The same held true when I went from half marathons to full marathons and then on to the ultra-distance.

While training for a half marathon (13.1 miles) I made a decision to run at my 10K (6.2 miles) pace. Around my sixth mile, I began running on empty. My lungs burned, my back hurt, and my legs were spent. I didn't see any way I could finish the race. I told myself to just run to the next aid station and quit. When I reached the table at the aid station, I grabbed a cup of water and a banana and told myself that once I'd finished them, I would quit.

Surprisingly, after the water and banana were in my system, I found myself still running—slower than I wanted but advancing. Then something happened. My breathing became less labored, my legs stopped aching, and my mind cleared. I had a second wind.

I began to run faster with less effort and I felt like I could run all day. I can't explain a second wind, but I know it's real.

The same is true in life and business when we find ourselves trying to stay in step with an ever-changing world. Seemingly the world just keeps spinning around faster and faster until we want to get off, or we're just hanging on for dear life. Technology advances faster than ever before and artificial intelligence is growing at a record pace. We are constantly connected, using up a chunk of our 1,440 daily minutes. Applications for our smart devices have changed us culturally and socially. Keeping pace is difficult. Too many times we quit or give up before we get our second wind.

Again, I have no idea how a second wind works. I just know second winds happen 100 percent of the time if we hang in there long enough for it to kick in. Since we don't know exactly when the second wind will kick into place, we must stay the course until it does.

The second wind works in every area of your life. I've seen it work in the personal, the financial, and the spiritual. The second wind has worked for me, so I know it will work for you!

What age are you? You might think, "I'm past the age of doing any of this stuff. My time has passed." When I turned fifty, a friend told me, "It's all downhill from here; you are now officially over the hill." My response: "Not if I find another hill to climb."

In my fifties, that's exactly what I did. I trained and ran a 50-mile race, I began a speaking career, I became an author, and I set a few personal-best sales years in real estate. I found my second wind. So can you! Keep going. Keep the pace.

DIG DEEP:

Where in your life have you struggled to keep up? What's one area where you need to speed up your pace and get in stride? Where are you falling behind and running at a slower pace? Pick one and don't give up because the second wind is coming.

We don't know when or we don't know how, we just know the second wind is coming. Once you get that second wind, things will become easier and more productive for you. How many times have you stopped just before the second wind? I've seen people at the dock waiting for their ship to come in. They get tired of waiting and leave just before their ship is docking. Someone else gets his or her ship. They missed the boat because they couldn't wait. Believe in the second wind. The second wind brings you to LifeAbundant365.

CHAPTER THIRTY-SEVEN:

Conquer Your Fear

For God has not given us a spirit of fear and timidity, but of power, love, and self-discipline. —2 Timothy 1:7 NLT

FROM YOUR FIRST BREATH until your last, fear is a constant threat, though it doesn't have to be. You can live a fear-free life.

What would living a fear-free life feel like? How would you do such a thing? How long will it take? When can I start? All are questions I've been asked once people began to dream of such a life.

When I taught my young son to swim, he could do all the things like kick his feet, submerge himself under the water, blow bubbles, and float on his back. But he always had to know that he was within reach of the pool's wall. If he had a finger or a toe connected to the pool wall, he was fearless. Removing that connection brought panic and fear. The same thing happened when I taught my daughter to ride her bike without training wheels. If I held the back of the bike's seat, she would be fine. However, once I let go, she would be afraid.

Jumping out of an airplane taught me a life lesson: You have to let go to conquer fear.

The minutes before you jump bring fear in the form of "what if?" Then the jumpmaster tells you, "You have ten seconds to jump on your own or I will help you with the first step!"

Once you jump, you have nothing to hold on to except your mind and what you must do next. Finally, you realize the fear that you had been feeling was unwarranted. You can do it.

I also learned that I was glad I only had ten seconds to decide to jump on my own. The best time to conquer fear is when it's small. Fear feeds and grows on time. The longer you wait, the bigger your fear becomes and the more difficult it is to conquer. You can't stay tethered to your safety line and experience the journey to your dream. You have to let go to grow. When you are about to attempt something new and you hesitate, fear arrives on your doorstep. This is the best time to destroy your fear. Attack it while it's small. Don't let it grow.

Most people's fear of loss is greater than their desire for gain. Such fear will block you from taking a chance at chasing your dreams. This fear will cause you to give in and give up, making fear the winner.

Fear distorts your perspective and causes you to see things from only the blurred view of fright. That can cause you to make poor decisions or paralyze you to make no decisions at all. Fear comes from the enemy, not from God. Fear wants to kill, steal, and destroy your dreams—and your life.

Just having a fear is the problem. Somewhere deep down, fear has taken you hostage and holds you back from living your life to your potential and catching your dreams. Fear—not the object of the fear—devours you.

Conquering fear requires the following:

- You must first confront your fear. Why are you afraid and how devastating is the fear to you?

- You must devise a plan to attack the fear. What are you losing because of the fear? What could you stand to gain if you weren't afraid?

- Take action. This is the most important step, even if it's just one small step forward. Taking action may be as simple as a phone call or an email making an appointment to move you away from fear and toward your dream.

"Inaction breeds doubt and fear. Action breeds confidence and courage. If you want to conquer fear, do not sit home and think about it. Go out and get busy." —Dale Carnegie

"If it scares you, it might be a good thing to try." —Seth Godin

DIG DEEP:

What do you fear the most and why? When did this fear take you hostage? What would it be like to release the bondage from your life? What would you gain if you conquered the fear in your life? What is the first step toward eliminating the fear?

CHAPTER THIRTY-EIGHT:
Escape the Herd

MY AUNT AND UNCLE OWNED a large farm in Kentucky. They had cows, chickens, horses, and many other animals. As a kid, I loved to go there in the summer. I learned many lessons from that farm that have shaped my life today.

Every evening the cows would make their way back to the barns. They always traveled the same path they had worn down after years of going back and forth. I marveled at their behavior. They call this the "herd mentality."

The cows were creatures of habit following the same path, at the same time, to the same place, every day. They did the same thing and got the same results. Sound familiar? Workers get up at the same time and drive the same way each day to arrive at the same job, then drive home at the end of the day. Examine the traffic around you on your next commute—it's a herd mentality. This may be fine for cows, but the creator of all things designed you to do more, be more, and have more, so you could serve more.

Insanity is doing the same thing over and over again and expecting a different outcome. The difference between where you are now and where you want to be can be found in your daily routine. Want different results? You'll need to take different actions. This is called the "science of achievement." When you take an action step, you'll get a result. Repeat that step and you'll repeat the result.

"We are what we repeatedly do." —Aristotle

Getting caught up in the herd mentality and taking the path of least resistance—a path to mediocrity—is far too easy. I understand the mentality, it's safe and easy. You just follow the herd at their slowed pace and you end up at their destination. If this ending is okay with you, stop reading this chapter and move on. If you want more, you must interrupt your current pattern. Ordinary people are products of their environment and fit in. Successful people change their environment and fly higher.

"If everyone is thinking alike, then somebody isn't thinking."
—George S. Patton

Thinking is becoming a lost art. The herd mentality has us following each other, copying the actions of others, and adopting their thoughts instead of thinking for ourselves. The tendency is for people's behavior and beliefs to conform to those of the group to which they belong. The practice of thinking and making decisions as a group is called "groupthink." Rejecting the group—learning to think and stand out on your own—is the only way to avoid groupthink. You must be different.

Take time to figure out who you are, what you want, and how you want to live your life. When you choose to be yourself and stick out, you'll attract friends who are truly like you—the real you. You'll also lose friends. Even some of your family may step back from you.

Thinking requires tuning out the noise and investing quiet time in deep thought and writing down your thoughts. Capture every thought on paper so you can begin to explore your thoughts and come up with the vital few things that are important to you. Everything begins with a thought, from the book you are reading to the device you use every day, they all started with a single thought. You may not understand how it works but you know it does. Thinking and not reacting is required to bust out of the herd.

You must actively define who you are, where you are, and what you truly want. The stronger your self-identity, the less others can influence you. You must also get comfortable with confrontation. When you start following your own thoughts over the path of the group, some of the group will come against you. This is normal. Expect it. Embrace it. Own it. Finally, you must trust yourself enough to stop blindly agreeing with the group. Keep on your own path. Not all will follow—and that's okay—you've just broken away from the herd. Keep going. You're on your way to the real you.

DIG DEEP:

Where have you been following the herd? When was the last time you invested in yourself by just deep thinking? Where do you really want to be? Where are you now? Be honest. Write down every thought even if you believe that's not possible. The best time to break away from the herd is now. The best way to break away from the herd is by regaining the power of deep thinking and taking action. Do it now!

CHAPTER THIRTY-NINE:
The Identity Shift

*"The two most important days in your life are the day you
are born and the day you find out why." —Mark Twain*

IS IT ANY WONDER we are confused about who we are? Think about
all of the seasons of identity change you have already gone through.
You were an elementary school kid, then a high schooler, and on to
college or the workforce for yet another change. I often hear folks
say, "Well, he/she is trying to find himself/herself." My problem has
always been that once I found myself, my season of life changed and
my identity shifted again. Joining the U.S. Air Force and the accompa-
nying change brought a major shift in my identity. Then I experienced
a culture shock when I left my Air Force career and jumped into my
new life as a civilian. My entire identity for twenty years had been that
of an active duty member of the U.S. Air Force.

We go from the identity of a young single adult to being married to
being a parent—many times in a handful of years. Talk about identity
shifting! And with the changes comes a time in our lives when we are

so busy being who our career, spouse, children, and community want and need us to be, we lose ourselves. It's one thing to catch a physical glimpse of ourselves in the mirror and say, "Who is that?" It's quite another thing to spend time alone thinking deep down. *Who am I really? What do I really want for the rest of my life?*

Why are you still here? What's your purpose in this life? Are you accomplishing your purpose? Can you accomplish your purpose where you are or will it require an "identity shift"?

An identity shift is choosing to change or adjust your current identity to fulfill a new season of life or, fulfill your purpose and experience a new season.

Some basic foundational rules for identity shifting are as follows:

- Our basic environment. We become a product of our environment. Living in the South, I've noticed that when a Northern boy or girl comes to the South, we'll have them speaking normally in just a few months.

- Our behavior. The people we hang around with the most influence us the most. We adapt to them. We take on their mannerisms and their line of reasoning.

- Habits. Our daily habits have consequences. Also, our habits are a hundred times stronger than our desires. We can want to have a change in our identity, but without a change in our habits, little else will change.

- Our beliefs and values. What we believe is important to us drives our action and inaction. Our beliefs can be self-limiting or unlimiting. It's up to us and what we focus on the most.

- Real change is internal, not external. So many times, I change the outside, but never the inside. This type of change will open the doors to groups and career opportunities, but it never lasts. Sooner or later you regret and despise living a lie. The saying

"Fake it till you make it" is a lie to yourself and rarely will you be able to continue the fake. "To thine own self be true."

All of these foundational truths develop or change our identity. Our internal peace is often disrupted by external circumstances. If we find ourselves in a new employment or social setting with values different from our own, we will experience conflict. Their values may be different than our own and we feel compelled to adapt and accept them for fear of losing our jobs, losing our friends, or of rejection. Even though on the inside we know it's wrong.

Our external circumstance becomes our new internal problem. We fit in with the group, but our new beliefs and actions betray our true values. So instead of feeling rejection and loss from others we now feel rejection and loss from self, which is worse by far.

Now we have a choice to make. We can take on their beliefs and values and make them our own, but in doing so, we lose our self to a new identity shift. Remember without discipline we become products of our environment. Or we can begin the identity-shift process and get back to the reason we were born. Get back to our purpose and our passion. Get back to being true to our self and authentic with others. In other words, start the process to find our true self and stop living a lie or a life of conflict.

"We are what we repeatedly do." —*Aristotle*

DIG DEEP:

Get to a quiet place with pen and journal in hand, then write the following: "Deep down inside who am I?" Really, who am I and what do I want to do and become from now until death? What values do I hold? What do I believe about this life? What is my passion? What are the most important things to me? How do I want to be remembered? What gifts do I have to perform to leave my little corner of the earth better than I found it? What is the best use of my time, talents, and treasures for the remainder of my life?

Now you're on your way to a new "Identity Shift" and this will help you live LifeAbundant365!

CHAPTER FORTY:
Empowered

WHEN I VISITED MY GRANDFATHER AS A KID, he would always ask, "Before you leave, please open six or seven cans of soup for me." His hands were arthritic and most days that made using the can opener too painful for him.

I would tell him, "Grandpa, I don't think it's healthy to leave cans of soup opened for days."

Finally, I purchased him an electric can opener and told him, "Now you can open all of the cans you want, whenever you need them."

A few months later, I stopped to visit Grandpa. When I got ready to leave, he said, "Hey, before you leave, please open six or seven cans of soup for me."

"Grandpa, just use the new opener I bought you," I said.

He replied, "That thing is harder to use than the old one."

We went to the kitchen and I got a can of soup and noticed the electrical cord on the opener was still wrapped up. I unwrapped it, plugged it in, and hit the lever to open the can. The motor made a noise and Grandpa asked, "What's that?"

"It's the electric motor," I said.

He'd been trying to use the opener like a handheld. Next, I had him open a can. He never had to request anyone to open a can for him after that.

Point being, everything he needed was at his fingertips: the soup, a stove, an appetite, a soup pan, a spoon, and a bowl. Everything he needed, but the power. He was operating on limited power—his own.

How about you? Where do you draw your power? Do you have everything you need, but lack the power? Are you operating at a deficit? If so, why? Many of us are running under limited power, which causes us to just get by. Why? Because of our limiting beliefs that control us. We could draw power from a friend or others we know if we would only ask them. Why don't we ask? Is it from pride or fear of rejection?

There is so much available to us in this age that none of us should ever act underpowered.

I believe in God the Father and I believe that Jesus through the Holy Spirit helps me operate from a position of power and authority when I'm plugged into Him. Maybe you believe this also, but haven't been plugged into the Lord recently. Or maybe you don't believe God and his power are available to you. Either way you are operating your life under your own limited power and beliefs. Your results will always be less than your potential. I don't share this belief to throw stones; I share it to help shed light on your current situation. Getting plugged in to the power will cause you to succeed at a higher level with less effort and with more accuracy.

DIG DEEP:

In what areas of your life could you use a boost? Where are you running on empty? What would some extra power do for you and your current life conditions? How could you receive some additional power right now? What's stopping you? Living a LifeAbundant365 is a powerful life!

CHAPTER FORTY-ONE:
Knowing vs. Doing

PLEASE, NEVER CONFUSE "knowing" with "doing." They are separate things altogether. We need to take more action, and we need to hear it. If this touches a nerve, please listen and make entries in your journal. Take some action!

While we all agree to become more successful, it's absolutely essential to continually learn and grow. However, all the knowledge in the world means nothing if you don't take action on it.

> *I do not understand what I do. For what I want to do I do not do, but what I hate I do. And if I do what I do not want to do, I agree that the law is good. As it is, it is no longer I myself who do it, but it is sin living in me. For I know that good itself does not dwell in me, that is, in my sinful nature. For I have the desire to do what is good, but I cannot carry it out. For I do not do the good I want to do, but the evil I do not want to do—this I keep on doing. Now if I do what I do not want to do, it is no longer I who do it, but it is sin living in me that does it. —Romans 7:15-20*

If you're not turning information you've learned into actions, the lessons are worthless. We only benefit from learning when we take action. Knowing how to cook will never feed us until we cook something. Knowledge alone is worthless to me. The power is in the doing.

I once lived in the space between knowing and doing. I always knew what I needed to do, yet I never could implement the lessons I'd learned into my daily life. I could always diagnose my problem—and I really wanted to do better—but applying change never happened for me.

When I lived in Knoxville, Tennessee, I ran a lot, which included running the thirteen miles from home to my office, then back home after work on Mondays, Wednesdays, and Fridays. Do the math. That translated to three marathons per week. On Tuesdays and Thursdays, I would take a long lunch and run from my office to the University of Tennessee and back. During one of those runs, I noticed a pack of UT runners just in front of me. I fell in behind them and became a part of the group, of which I had twelve years on the oldest member.

One afternoon while running with the UT group, we turned onto the campus and within minutes they darted up a steep, grassy hill. I tried to follow, but when I reached the top of the hill, all I could see was the last runners making a turn and disappearing from sight. I'd been left in their dust, gasping for air. This episode made me angry with myself, so I began hill training on Mondays, Wednesdays, and Fridays instead of making my daily office commute. And I trained as hard as I ever had trained. Weeks later, I felt ready when I reached the bottom of the hill with the group. Accordingly, I attacked the hill only to be passed and left behind again. Training alone wouldn't work against youth and superior athleticism.

I'd always known that I couldn't outrun a bad diet. My motto back then was "Eat to Run, Run to Eat!" I loved sugar, desserts, fried foods, and cheeseburgers with fries. Pizza twice a week was simply carb loading. My poor diet ran counter to the knowledge I possessed that fruits, vegetables, and a lot of water would improve my running performance. Better nutrition would have helped bridge the gap between aging and athleticism and would have allowed me to perform much better. Yet

I didn't get it. That left me in the uncomfortable position of being stationed between knowing how to improve my current life conditions and actually doing so.

Knowing is one thing. Doing is what makes things happen. Doing is what puts knowledge into motion. Doing is what makes your goals a reality. Doing is the benefit of knowing. Doing is what allows you to live a LifeAbundant365. Never confuse knowing for doing. You must implement what you've learned to make it valuable and to really benefit from it.

How do we go from just knowing what we should do to start doing it? The simple answer is to interrupt the pattern of not doing. You know what to do. Not doing it is just a habit. You are in the habit of not doing. You must break the habit.

Neuroplasticity is the ability of the brain to change its physical structure and function through thought, emotion, and activity. It's within your power to rewire your brain to do what you need to do. You must practice the action of thinking and acting on your thoughts and emotions.

The following offers a few ways to expedite the process of breaking habits:

- Recognize and acknowledge you have the habit of not doing.
- Develop a new habit to replace the bad habit of not doing. When you catch yourself not doing something you know you should be acting on—stop!
- Take the first step to doing. Just taking the first step is the beginning of a new habit.
- Repeat taking the first step every time you recognize the old habit and then add taking whatever the next step is, too. Eventually you will unconsciously take action on the knowledge you have when the opportunity arises.

DIG DEEP:

Where in your life are you not acting on the knowledge you have? It could be your diet or exercise program. You might know you need to get out of debt, or you need to save money, yet you're not doing it. Just think about the possibilities if we stopped doing stupid stuff and began doing what we already know to do. We would be living a Life-Abundant365.

CHAPTER FORTY-TWO:
Success Is Hard to Handle

I'VE EXPERIENCED FAILURES AND SUCCESSES. Through those experiences, I've concluded that success is more difficult to manage. Because I had failed more often than I had succeeded, that experience felt more familiar. Failure brought the expectation that I would fail several times before I succeeded—it's a process.

In order to be a success, you must get comfortable with failure. Failure is not quitting. I put myself in position to fail often just to gain experience and learn new things. I realized that failure was part of the process toward success.

Ever watch a newly born foal try to stand and walk? Or ever see a baby taking his or her first steps? They wobble and stagger around completely off balance. They try and try and fail and fail until they finally take several consecutive steps on their own. How many times should a parent allow their healthy child to attempt walking before they say, "Just quit, it's too hard for you"?

Never, right?

Failure is the best instructor. If you aren't failing you aren't trying. Failure is a measuring stick of my effort and activity. It's how I can see my progress.

I remember learning to play golf. We took a family vacation to Hilton Head and our hotel sat next to a golf academy attached to a beautiful golf course. Being there allowed me to sign up for a week of lessons.

They videoed my swing while I hit balls into a video screen. One of the golf professionals offered me an evaluation. "Mr. Day, after a thorough review of your golf skills, we have determined that you have so many things wrong and so many bad habits that we can't help you much in one week. However, we do feel comfortable that we can make you efficient in one or two things. What would you most like instruction on?"

"Driving the ball!" I said.

We worked on teeing off with the driver. By the end of the week I had built so much confidence that to this day I don't get anxious teeing off in front of groups. I'm no Tiger Woods, but I can consistently make good contact and hit a respectable shot.

Success is less familiar to us because we have more experience with failure. Success changes you while much around you doesn't change. You may have a successful career move or promotion or write a successful book or maybe start up a successful business while your friends and extended family members remain the same. Nothing changed for them, but you changed.

Having success builds momentum and paves the way for even greater success. Your attitude improves and your lifestyle may upgrade. Maybe you can afford a new car, wardrobe, or a new house. Now you can travel more and take your family on nice trips. Maybe you buy a vacation house at a lake or beach. All are good things if you have the discipline to remain humble and maintain your balance of life. You must guard your heart against pride because pride comes before the fall.

The harder you work, the more successful you become. But success comes at a price. Your responsibilities increase and people become dependent on you for their livelihood, which puts more pressure and stress on you. You work harder to keep up and you become more detached from your family and friends.

When I first retired from the U.S. Air Force and began my real estate career, I had a conversation with a veteran real estate agent. He asked me, "What is your objective for your real estate practice?" I told him, "I want to make $250,000 per year!" He looked at me with a serious face and said, "You want to make $250,000 a year and I have to make $250,000 a year just to pay my bills! Don't ever get to where I am." Sound counsel. I assured him I wouldn't get to that point.

Within five years my lifestyle had changed dramatically. I found myself giving my family all the things I wasn't able to give them on an Air Force income. The more success I had, the more I upgraded our lifestyle and the busier and the more detached I became. At the brink, I had seven companies and worked nonstop. I couldn't enjoy the fruits of my labor. My stress level went off the charts, I had high blood pressure and I became demanding. I wanted to do more, be more, and have more. Exactly what I didn't need—more of everything.

I believe unbridled success has destroyed more marriages, families, and people than failure ever did.

DIG DEEP:

Where in your life are you positioned for failure in order to improve the opportunity for future success? What is your plan to control and handle success when it happens? What conversations are you having consistently with your family as you gain success? The key to being successful is communication with your family and friends. Also giving appropriate time to each equity of your life: Family, Faith, Friends, Health, Financial. LifeAbundant365 means giving while you are living!

CHAPTER FORTY-THREE:

Worry? What Is It Good For? Absolutely Nothing!

DEPENDING ON WHO YOU BELIEVE, the life span for an average person is seventy-eight years. Of note, twenty-eight of those years are spent sleeping. And as many as seven of those sleeping years are spent lying awake with worry about family, career, money, retirement, crime, politics, health, friends, relationships, the unknown, and about a million other things.

Reflecting on my life, I wish I'd worried less. Worrying isn't worth the cost of stress, lost sleep, fatigue, problems, loss of energy, feelings of helplessness. After all, most of what we worry about never happens.

So, why do we worry?

I believe I did so to help solve my problems or challenges in life. I would try and think of everything that could go wrong. Worrying was my attempt at controlling and solving my problems. I believed that worrying would help me think through each one and control the outcome. It didn't.

When my daughter first started driving, she had a few minor accidents. One evening she went out with friends and she was the driver. I had gone to bed early, only to have my wife wake me later. "Something is wrong! She may have had an accident!"

Our daughter had not answered her cell phone and hadn't responded to text messages. I told my wife our daughter was fine. "She's probably having fun and not checking her phone. You worry too much."

When I tried to go back to sleep, my mind shifted to overdrive. *She has had a few accidents. She is with her friends and they may be talking, laughing, and listening to music and not paying attention while driving.*

I got out of bed and rushed into the sunroom where my wife sat. I told her, "Don't just sit there, start calling the hospitals and her friends—she could be lying in a ditch!"

Minutes later, our daughter checked in and all was fine. Most of what we worry about never happens!

So, how do we stop worrying so much?

After decades of worrying, I realized that almost none of what I had worried about happened. When potential worrisome situations arose in the future, I reminded myself of my epiphany about worrying. I learned to substitute worry with another activity, like reading. If I caught myself beginning to worry about something, I would read a book. Reading would move my mind toward something positive and I would repeat to myself.

"Do not be anxious about anything." —Philippians 4:16

Never google your worry. For example, inquiring about your symptoms on one of the medical sites. You'll quickly conclude that you have two weeks to live. Then you'll really have something to worry about!

Worrying about your health can make you unhealthy. Worrying about the health of people you care about will drive you crazy. No matter what your circumstances are, begin to practice good health tactics. Begin to eat better and move more. Drink more water and get in the sun a few minutes per day. Talk with medical folks and others on the same pathway as you. Get help!

Worry's best friend is anxiety. Anxiety can cause serious medical problems when allowed to run wild in your mind. Little bad things can turn into big bad things if left unchecked. Take control of your worry while it's small. The outcome of any situation is never determined by how much you worry about it.

One of the best ways to stop thinking about yourself and your worries is to help someone else with their problems and worries. You'll quickly realize how small some of your problems really are.

DIG DEEP:

Where in your life do you worry too much? Why? How much of what you worry about becomes reality? Where do you need to stop worrying and take action? What must you do to stop worrying? Begin to tell yourself, "I'm not worrying about this today, I will worry about it tomorrow." Remember nothing and no one is perfect. Eliminating worry from your life will have you living a LifeAbundant365! Don't worry, be happy!

CHAPTER FORTY-FOUR:
Extraordinary Routines and Habits

WE ARE CREATURES OF HABIT. Habits are a hundred times stronger than desires. No amount of willpower and desire will ever trump a habit in the long term. Sooner or later you will return to the default habit unless the old habit is replaced by a new one.

Take a diet. You can be doing great for weeks on a well-planned diet. Then one day you wake up and you no longer feel like being on a diet. All you want is a cheat day. No problem, right? What's one day? A few days later you don't feel like it again and you skip another day then another, and before you know it you are back into your old habits and routines.

What happened?

You wanted to lose weight and you needed to lose weight. Your well-planned diet was even working. You just didn't change your habit first and you need an extraordinary routine.

Extraordinary routines are subtle changes done over a period of time that result in big changes and form good habits. Good habits hold the power to guide you through the "I don't feel like it" days.

Extraordinary routines are critical because you already have a daily routine you follow without a second thought. Whether it's waking up and checking your phone or getting into the shower, then grabbing that first cup of coffee. Good or bad, you unconsciously follow your routine every day—it's a habit!

Be aware of these habits. They are your constant companions and your future life conditions. If you don't want to be controlled by your habits, you must control them. Take an inventory of your current habits and routines. Which ones do you need to replace and why?

How do I implement extraordinary routines or habits into my life? Clarity is a good beginning. Send a clear message to your mind about what you want to accomplish and why. Your brain is designed to help you reach your objective by filtering out the things you aren't looking for and focusing on the things you are looking for. Your Reticular Activating System—RAS—becomes sensitive to what you want and brings that to your attention. You help feed your RAS by thinking about your desires, writing them down, talking about them, and continuing to send a consistent message to your mind.

To generate more energy, develop the habit of taking more breaks throughout the day. You must take a break every hour. Leave your desk or your office for fifteen minutes and simply walk around the parking lot. Grab a cup of coffee. Talk with friends or co-workers. Clear your mind. When you return to your task, you will have better energy and get more accomplished.

You must master your craft to become extraordinary in your field of expertise. What must you do to become an expert? How do you rank in the top 20 percent, then 15 percent, to the top 5 percent in your specialty? Eliminate tasks or jobs that can be outsourced or eliminated. We have become a busy, but mediocre, society. Lose the distractions. Focus on the vital few things that really move the needle. We could accomplish more in every area of life if we would just eliminate distractions. This requires extraordinary routines, discipline, and habits.

Distractions come in all shapes and sizes. They can cause us to lose attention for a few minutes, hours, or days. The best way to remain focused is to be ready to say "no" or "not now." Your time is valuable and everyone wants some of it. The more successful you become, the more of you people want. I've learned a script that goes something like this: "I'm sorry, but I will have to say no on your offer to meet today." Or maybe: "Not now, but I can meet tomorrow." You must develop the habit of respecting your time and attention. Nobody else will.

Soon your reputation will become known and your value in the marketplace will increase.

DIG DEEP:

Take an inventory of your habits and routines. Where do you need a change? What new habits and routines do you need to establish to become extraordinary? What little things can you start today and keep going even when you don't feel like it? These new habits and routines will make you more successful and you will begin to enjoy LifeAbundant365!

CHAPTER FORTY-FIVE:
Are You a Chameleon?

A CHAMELEON TURNS BROWN on brown sand. On green grass, it turns green. A chameleon blends in with its surroundings. The desire to blend in is normal and natural wherever you are. We all want to belong.

Toward the end of summer, I'll notice parents running around the local stores doing back-to-school shopping for their children. They are looking for the trendy stuff—backpacks, shoes, clothes, technology devices—so their kids can be like the other kids. They've reached a point where they can't pick their kids out of a crowd. They blend in.

Adults are the same way. Men and women search for the things that make them blend in with the rest of their world. They'll mimic the dominant group at work just to be accepted.

The need to be accepted is a basic human instinct. Nobody wants to become an anonymous clone without such acceptance. Some people have different versions of themselves at work, home, play, or online. Are you being accepted for who you really are or some fake other version of yourself?

We try to impress others by what we say, do, drive, and wear. We make decisions based on what others are saying and doing instead of following our own desires and inner voice. Going along to get along is easier than being an exception. We take the comfortable path to blend in so we don't draw attention to ourselves. This path eventually will feel normal even though deep inside we know it's not really us. We are living a lie. We want to avoid rejection at all cost, but in doing so, we may very well become rejected by ourselves.

You were created to stand out—not blend in! You have gifts and talents that you and others need. Being different from the crowd is okay. We invest so much time and money on dressing up the outside that we are neglecting the most important part of each of us, the inside.

What really matters is the inside. The inside will always show up on the outside no matter what we are wearing. Sooner or later the real you will break through to the outside. Many times, this happens much later in life after we have convinced ourselves that our time has passed. But rest assured, it's never too late.

What others are saying or doing won't matter to you at some point in your life. You'll finally understand that what others think about you is none of your business. Getting released from the bondage of blending in allows us to discover true freedom. We are all different and play an important part in our relationships, family, work, community, and everywhere we go. People should see a difference in you without staring. You have a lot to offer.

"Just be yourself" is a cliché, but one that holds true. Being yourself means having the courage to accept yourself. After all, just being you is enough. Accepting who you really are, with all of your flaws and challenges, is no small task. However, that acceptance will eventually become normal to you. Remember: nobody's perfect.

People want to be around people they know, like, and trust. If you're not authentic and real, they lose trust in you. Being so many versions of yourself is exhausting. Eventually you will crash and burn. All of your efforts to blend in to be accepted will be lost in the crash, causing people to dismiss you from their lives and putting you on the outside looking in. All because you just wanted to be accepted. Be yourself. That's the person everybody wants to know.

DIG DEEP:

Think about your life. Do you act one way with this group and another way with that group? Does your social media portray the real version of you or a different one? You must define who you are and become your inner self. While that can be a daunting task—because we all want to fit in and be accepted—it's time for you to be accepted for who you really are.

CHAPTER FORTY-SIX:
Living a LifeAbundant365 Kick-Starters

*"Those who have been truly converted to Jesus Christ know
the meaning of 'abundant living.'" —Billy Graham*

THE PURPOSE OF THIS BOOK and your journaling is about how to capture more abundance in your day-to-day, "ordinary common" life. The first step to LifeAbundant365 is to be rooted to Jesus.

Here is a list of kick-starters to abundant living:

- Invest some time thinking and writing in your journal the little things that bring you pleasure in life. Then, seek these little things daily. A few of my favorite little things are: Drinking a fresh cup of coffee in the early morning and thinking about my blessings, such as my wife, my children, and my grandchildren. I give thanks for each one.
- Reading your Bible. This always calms me and makes me thankful.
- Walking for ten minutes in the sun. I take a few breaks throughout the day to walk around my parking lot, letting the sun hit my face as I go.

- Brief thinking sessions. I love to retreat to a quiet spot with my thoughts and journal. At those moments, I think about what I want in the near and distant future. Writing down my thoughts gets me excited and energized. These brief sessions last about fifteen minutes. The results are life changing.

Next, develop and implement good habits. Little bad habits turn into big bad habits and little good habits turn into big good habits. So, I try to be intentional with forming little good habits. A few basic, but powerful habits are:

- Anything you do, do with your absolute best effort. If I have too many things to do, I can't do anything with my absolute best effort. Thus, I keep a short "do" list and I keep it simple. I don't overcommit myself, so when I have a task to accomplish, I can give it my absolute best. I stay focused on the mission and work hard while I'm working and I play hard when I'm at play. Don't mix work with play. The word here is "focus."

- You must take responsibility for your current life conditions. Your habits create your own reality. Start fresh today. Take action to initiate a new habit to improve your future life conditions. These may include self-improvement, reading more, attending a seminar, listening to a podcast, or seeking out a mentor to help you grow.

- Develop a habit of practicing good financial health. Save money and get out of debt. We all know what to do, the problem is we don't do it. Your financial future depends on your present choices. Start small right where you are and begin with the facts of your income and your expenses. Identify where you can cut expenditures. Set a budget. Discipline is required. Sacrifice now so you can have more and do more later.

- Develop a habit of practicing good physical health. Eat right, exercise, and drink more water. Most of us know what to do where health choices are concerned—we just don't consistently do them. This is one of the greatest areas to implement little subtle good habits.

Gain clarity by sending a clear message to your mind on what you want and who you want to become. Deep-thinking sessions will be required. You must discover what you truly want for your life and take action. Energy grows where your focus goes. Don't waste energy on the things you don't want.

DIG DEEP:

Grab your journal, get to a quiet space, and evaluate these points. Allow yourself to think. Write down your thoughts. Choose one or two ideas—the vital few—and focus on them. These ideas coupled with deep thinking will develop into an action plan for change. Words like commitment, self-control, discipline, and consistency are all part of your plan for improvement. These little steps will soon have you on the path to LifeAbundant365.

CHAPTER FORTY-SEVEN:
You Can Handle It

*"Whether you think you can, or you think
you can't—you're right." —Henry Ford*

WHATEVER YOU THINK YOU CAN'T HANDLE, you're most likely wrong—you can. Just when you think you can't go on and you're out of gas, you find a full-reserve tank.

You have more strength, more resilience, and more wisdom than you give yourself credit for having. Mind over matter makes you stronger than you think.

As I've stated earlier, I love endurance racing and that love prompted me to run in marathons and ultramarathons. Many people have asked me how I could run those distances. Some have joked, "I don't like to drive my car that far!"

Mind over matter, that's how.

Our bodies are miraculous creations that adapt to most conditions. Normally, our body is not the first one to quit, that distinction belongs to our mind. We must convince our mind that we are not quitting no matter what. You are in control. One foot in front of the other is the method.

Don't underestimate the power of your mind, whether it's for you or against you. The mind is a powerful force that doesn't just work on you physically and mentally, it tries to control every aspect of your life.

In relationships, the unbridled mind will cause you to be jealous, easily offended, and quick to judgment. The mind will want you to take the easy path and quit. A thought starts the process.

In business, an uncontrolled mind will cause the same emotions as in relationships and can cause rebellion and a negative attitude. Again, the mind will want you to take the path of least resistance and resign.

Controlling your mind is essential. Taking every thought captive is the quickest way to do that. A negative thought about quitting or being offended must be replaced with a positive thought. We can only think one thought at a time. Think positive. Once you identify a negative thought, you must swat it away like a wasp that just landed on your nose. Brush it off and move fast to a positive thought before you get stung.

Perception is not reality. We may look at a challenge or situation and perceive that it is impossible for us to handle. Big problems can bring big anxiety if we allow that to happen. Breaking down the problem into small, easy to-do steps delivers the solution. All of our thoughts must focus on the solution and not the problem or challenge. If you catch a negative thought in your mind, use this tactic of controlling your thoughts. You will regain control, capture peace of mind, restore your memory, and have sleep-filled nights. Where focus goes, energy flows.

If your mind allows fear, doubt, worry to run wild, please understand these are not from God, but the enemy.

Satan, you are a liar. I will not receive (or believe) your lie in the Name of Jesus. —2 Corinthians 10:5

Finally, brothers, whatever is true, whatever is honorable, whatever is just, whatever is pure, whatever is lovely, whatever is commendable, if there is any excellence, if there is anything worthy of praise, think about these things. —Philippians 4:8 (ESV)

You must become aware of your thoughts and take action either for or against them. A negative mind will not allow you to have a positive, exciting life. If you struggle with negative thinking, you must come to terms with the fact that your life won't change until the way you think does. Nobody is strong enough to reason with their mind. We must control it and renew it constantly. A weak mind will never lead you to a strong, powerful, and abundant life.

> *A calm and undisturbed mind and heart are the life and health of the body, but envy, jealousy, and wrath are like rottenness of the bones.*
> *—Proverbs 14:30*

Having experienced a wandering mind and a controlled one, I have concluded that nothing in your life will ever operate at Level 10 until your mind is. Today is the day to set your mind. The toughest part of any competition you enter will take place in your mind. If you are not strong, you will lose this internal conflict. Negative self-talk is the secret tactic against us. We must set our minds on Level 10 to claim victory in this arena.

DIG DEEP:

With your journal open and pen in hand, read back through this chapter and make notes on your strengths and weaknesses. Choose one weakness you need to work on immediately, then take the first step to eliminating it. You are well on your way to living a LifeAbundant365!

CHAPTER FORTY-EIGHT:
A Fresh Start

MAYBE YOU'VE QUIT A JOB or a relationship—perhaps you were let go or released not by your choice. In any case, starting over requires a leap of faith along with courage and endurance to face your new future.

Emotions run high while energy and motivation can run low. While there's the excitement of new opportunities and the coming adventure, there's also insecurity and the fear of failure looming in your mind.

Too many times we have regrets or refuse to forgive ourselves for our past mistakes and choices. We must deal with what happened so we can move on. What's past is past.

Taking inventory of what happened to end the situation is the first step toward discerning where things went wrong, why they failed, and what part did you play in it. The objective is to learn from the experience. That awareness will help you avoid making the same mistake while also helping you to remove any regret and blame. Resolving your issue prevents it from affecting your future. This inventory and review should be brief and concise. The objective is to get a clear picture of the problem, solve it, and move on with your life.

Maybe you are just in a rut and need motivation to get back in the game. Everybody hits a bump in the road at one time or another. We need to set our minds on the good things ahead for us. New beginnings can be full of excitement, momentum, and enthusiasm if we see it that way. Our perspective plays a huge part in a fresh start.

The next step may sound strange, but it's essential: Be selfish for a season.

To really start fresh, focus on you. Many of us are so busy helping everyone around us that we have a tendency to neglect ourselves at the expense of our physical, financial, or mental health. This is the time to give you the best chance of succeeding at what's next. Your best effort is required. Rest, therapy, alone time, a change of scenery, or being around people that will encourage you could all be a part of the equation at this point. This is an important time for you to prepare yourself to become all you can be and live a LifeAbundant365.

Decide what type of fresh start you desire and need. What will it take to launch a fresh start? Knowing what you want in life makes it easier to take action. Knowing why you want the fresh start makes it sustainable. Remember, for this short season the reboot of your life is all about you. Life has no pause button. No matter what happens, life keeps spinning on. Life does have a reboot button. You just have to locate it and push reboot to restart your life.

Two power tools in life are time and energy.

Protecting your time takes incredible effort. There is no such thing as saving time. When the clock strikes midnight a new day begins, along with your daily allotment of 1,440 minutes. Once these precious minutes are spent, they never return. Use your time wisely.

You need an enormous amount of energy to get you to where you want to be. Results and momentum fuel that energy. The more successful you become, the more energetic you become. Neglecting to use your time wisely will drain your energy, as will being surrounded by energy-sucking people, who want to see you back with them and not moving on to your fresh start. Be alert and take action to remove yourself from those people. They are running on empty and you are fueled by the high octane of a fresh start.

Sculpting the art of a fresh start in my life has taken years. Failures and rejections are inescapable. The more you live, the more opportunity you have to start over. You can't change the past, but you can change direction right now. If we allow the bad times to win, they seem to build on one another and pile up on us. But if we look at each week as a fresh start to try and go in a different direction, the fresh starts soon outnumber the bad.

Make a bucket list of all the things you really want to do with your life. Maybe traveling to exotic places, learning a new language, completing your education, starting your own business, making an impact on something bigger than you (like a charity), or running for political office. Live your life to the fullest. Don't settle. Why not you? A thought starts the process followed by an action step, and suddenly you are that much closer to living your dreams. You can always find the time and a way if you focus your energy in that direction. You can do it.

I love Mondays! They are a fresh start to a new business week. A chance to forget what's behind and to press onward toward the prize. I tell the groups at my speaking events: "Remember to always try to get something from the day. Don't just try to get through the day. The world is happening for you, not to you!" When you feel overwhelmed, just take a step back and start again. You have everything it takes to be successful.

DIG DEEP:

Where in your life have you had a failure or a setback? Why did it happen? What did you learn from it? Set that experience free to live in the past where it belongs. Make it a distant memory and start fresh today. Walk through the steps we discussed in this chapter and begin anew. You have a lot of life to live. Live it Abundantly 365!

CHAPTER FORTY-NINE:
Think Big

I NEED TO TALK TO YOU as your coach for a chapter. Stay with me. Keep an open mind, open ears, and a willing heart.

The biggest limits we have in our life usually are self-inflicted. In order to break through the ordinary and live your big dreams, you must crush those self-imposed limitations and limiting beliefs. Now, hang on to your hat while facing this difficult task that requires a level of discomfort on your part. Buckle up and try to find satisfaction in the uncomfortable. Believe me, that is possible.

Much of my military training was new to me initially, particularly the physical and mental challenges I faced as a warrior trainee. Every day came down to a binary choice of attack and beat the challenge or fail and wash out of training. No other options or do-overs were available. Talk about uncomfortable. Eventually, I found comfort in high levels of discomfort. I know that sounds strange, but the more breakthroughs you have during the discomfort, the more comfortable you become with the process. You have to stay the course. Don't settle or lower the dream or goal. Raise it.

Scheduling time to think big is the first critical step to thinking big. This time must be free of all distractions. The first couple of sessions should last about fifteen minutes. You should eventually work your way up to thirty, sixty, ninety minutes. Just you, a pen, and a journal. Write down every thought you have. Think bigger and bigger. Your thoughts should surprise and even scare you. Use your imagination. Don't stop. Keep going. The more you think, the more ideas, strategies, and tactics you will develop. No small thinking during this session. Just focus on big dreams. Just focus on what seems impossible to you.

> *"Once you have mastered time, you will understand how true it is that most people overestimate what they can accomplish in a year —*
> *and underestimate what they can achieve in two or three decades!"*
> *—Tony Robbins*

Breakthroughs happen one step at a time over a long period of time. Consistency and perseverance are required, meaning you'll need self-discipline and you'll also need others to push you along the path. Enlist friends who believe in you when you won't. Now is the time to set huge, long-term goals to work toward.

I've always dreamed big. I call it "day dreaming" because it's all about me. I can go from deep thinking to deep doing. The best tip I can give you is to remove "can't" from your vocabulary and remove the naysayers from your life. Breakthroughs are difficult enough.

There are so many tricks to get you through the tough spots. Celebrate the little wins along the way. Enjoy the "Ta-Da" moments. When we have little children around us, they always want to show you their moves or breakthroughs, such as a dance move, their ABC's, a song, etc. After they perform, they stand tall and proclaim, "Ta-Da!" They are rejoicing and we applaud and celebrate their accomplishments with them. Somewhere along the way we lose this special celebration.

At some of my speaking events, I have asked everyone to stand and yell, "Ta-Da!" Doing so affords a moment to remember what accomplishment feels like, even in a small win. The exercise never fails to bring a smile to my face. Theirs too!

DIG DEEP:

What is one big thing you really want to accomplish? Remember this big thing may take a longer period of time to complete, but you are winning all along the way. What is the big thing, and what is the first action step needed to start you along the way? Remember you aren't asking your friends and family for permission to win big. You're just asking for their support and encouragement. Some will say it's impossible or you'll never do it. Ignore them. Just keep winning and celebrating. You are on your way to winning big and living a LifeAbundant365!

CHAPTER FIFTY:
Creating a Wealth Mindset

They are always thinking about how much it costs. "Eat and drink," they say, but they don't mean it. —Proverbs 23:7

I LIVE BY THE SAYING "What you think about, you bring about!"

As a Man Thinketh is a self-help book by James Allen published in 1903. Inspired by the abovementioned Proverbs scripture, I read Allen's book twice every year because it deals with the power of thought. The book portrays that each of us in our own thought world holds the key to every life condition, good or bad. And by working intelligently upon our thoughts, it's possible to recreate our life, and transform our current and future life conditions.

Many would define wealth as monetary or material accumulation, but being wealthy isn't all about money. Wealth is about overall well-being, abundance, having time, success, and the right mindset.

We must not only have wealth in our financial life, we must also have wealth in our spiritual, personal, physical, and professional lives. LifeAbundant365 requires the proper mindset.

Even the best thoughts are nothing more than wishes if you don't apply action to them. Let's say a great idea hits you and you sit in your recliner for a few hours talking and thinking about it. Several days pass and you are still just thinking about your great idea, but not doing anything about it. That renders the thought worthless. Hoping and wishing are not doing.

To develop the wealth in any area of your life you desire, you have to put in massive action to receive massive results. That means eliminating the actions, the habits, and the behaviors that are holding you back. Then you must implement the actions, the habits, and the behaviors that move you forward toward the wealth mindset.

This chapter is designed to create abundant wealth in your whole life. Here are some practical ways you can start attracting wealth and success in your own life:

Invest in yourself. Never stop learning and growing. The rapid pace of technological change along with all of the other societal changes dictate that you must continue improving your knowledge base and skill set. If you don't, you will become obsolete, like pay phones and transistor radios. Learning is an ongoing process you must continue to increase your value in the marketplace. There is no "I made it" and no "done." Life is defined by challenges and learning.

Focus on the top priority for today. Given the fast-paced, action-packed, busy world we live in, you can easily get distracted by an urgent, but unimportant task. Ask yourself every day, "What is the objective of my future?" Then write down, "What absolutely must get done today?" Focus your energy on the must-get-done list. Apply massive action toward reaching your target. You can do this because you are working on a few targets, not lists of multiple tasks. The ability to focus is the key to success.

Scarcity-vs.-abundance mindset. So many people say they want wealth, prosperity, and abundance yet they only have a scarcity mindset. When I teach this topic while spending time with groups, I find minds filled with worry about bills and lack of money. They think along the lines of either/or, but never both. If you're living in a scarcity mindset, you always think that your money will run out. A scarcity mindset is focused on lack. Accordingly, that harbors thoughts about what you don't have instead of what you truly want, which is wealth. Remember, what you think about, you bring about! In order to turn this perception around, make it a point to see the abundance that surrounds you. Be grateful for the money and job you do have. Believe and proclaim that you will receive more money soon. Believe you can improve your life and make more money. Take action to build wealth in every area of your life (do something every day). And develop a plan and execute it today. Why not you?

> *"Driven by the fear of loss and uncertainty of the future, the masses focus on how to protect and hoard their money. While world-class thinkers understand the importance of saving and investing, they direct their mental energy toward accumulating wealth through serving people and solving problems."* —Steve Siebold

Again, your focus is the key to your future. By investing your time-talent-treasure into every area of your life, you will become richer than you ever dreamed. Apply massive mental energy toward the wealth mindset and believe it can happen for you. Focus on what you want and how you can serve others or solve a problem in the marketplace. Then believe. Your beliefs will always prove you right.

A wealth mindset is developed by those who invest time thinking about every area of their life. I would estimate that wealthy people think about how to best improve the equities of their life up to twenty-five hours per month. Then they execute their thoughts.

DIG DEEP:

Are you operating from a mindset of scarcity or abundance? Why? What do you really want? Stop "fixing to" and start doing. Your future is up to you. Hoping and wishing will not work. You must apply massive action on your target. Only then will you receive massive results. Living a LifeAbundant365.

CHAPTER FIFTY-ONE:
Handling Criticism

NONE OF US LIKE to be criticized.

Think about the last time that you got a compliment and then think about the last time you were criticized. What hit you harder and stayed with you longer?

Criticism can make you feel attacked and judged all in one punch to the gut. "Consider the source" of the criticism is normally your best defense followed by "What do they know?" and "Who cares what they think?" Then we replay the criticism over and over in our minds, sharing the criticism with our friends while looking for something to prove them wrong.

> *"Any fool can criticize, condemn, and complain but it takes character and self-control to be understanding and forgiving."*
> —*Dale Carnegie, How to Win Friends and Influence People*

Do you have room in your imagination where you can embrace criticism from anyone regardless of why they attacked you? Great room for growth exists within each of us. The catalyst for that growth may come from an unlikely source: the critic.

I have received my fair share of criticism—some constructive and some destructive. Through my experience, I have attained the skill set of "handling criticism." I've successfully used my learned skill set throughout the past decade. If you apply this to your life, it will work for you, too.

First and foremost, you should stay calm and hear the critic out. Never retaliate, cut them off, or speak over them. Allow them their fifteen minutes of fame and calmly listen until they've finished. Acknowledge their comment without getting defensive. Simply say you will have to think about what they have said.

Why this approach?

Because many times I have quickly responded only to regret my words the next day. I let my feelings get in the way. You should never base decisions on feelings. Perhaps there is a shred of constructive truth in their criticism. Time in this situation is your friend. Take some time to evaluate.

A man who refuses to admit his mistakes can never be successful.
—Proverbs 28:13

Ask yourself why the criticism was made? Don't automatically think the critic is right, but don't automatically think the critic is wrong. Take time to evaluate for yourself. Is there a nugget of truth in the criticism? Can you improve with a minor tweak here or there? Even if the critic is 99 percent wrong, the critic is still 1 percent right. Use the 1 percent to your advantage.

My second assignment in the U.S. Air Force was with a tough-minded outfit of elite warriors. Our motto was: "Thin of skin need not come in." Sixty-four of the most ruthless guys I have ever known. They were also relentless in many ways. They took their business seriously and you needed to make sure you weren't the weak link. If you did something sub-par, you would immediately suffer a fury of comments, criticisms, and name-calling. They expected the best from themselves and also from you. Their lives could hinge on you performing. They were true brothers. We could say and do things to each other because we were brothers, but we would never permit the same from any outsiders. When one member had a need of any kind, sixty-three warriors would be the solution, regardless of challenge. The criticism they levied cut to the chase and was designed to make you better. They may not like you, but they would lay down their life for you. Embracing their criticism always led to improvement.

After one of my speaking events I received a criticism that was cutting and devastating to my ego.

I had been speaking for a couple of years and I had developed a style and skill that I felt comfortable using. I wrote a session for a large company and practiced presenting it for a couple of weeks. I felt prepared and confident. After my presentation, I reviewed my performance in my mind and decided I had reached a new level. The presentation had been my best ever.

About a week later, I received a survey back from the chief operating officer that stated how "dissatisfied and disappointed" he had been in my keynote speech. I was shocked and annoyed.

I read the survey again from the beginning. Maybe I'd misread it. "Dissatisfied and disappointed" it said. "What does he know?" I muttered. I spent hours on that presentation. What did he expect? I'd delivered exactly what they had requested.

A few days passed and I called him. I had to. His words continued to sting. I had never been told anything like that. During the call he told me I had great content and he could tell I had been well prepared. However, he thought I'd come across as though I wanted the audience to like me and be impressed with me. He that he believed I had the potential to be the best speaker he had ever heard (and he had heard some incredible speakers) if I would take the focus off me and place it on the audience. Just disregard the speaker and focus them on the message.

We talked for an hour. After the call, I thought about how much of what he said was true. I wanted to be the best speaker so badly I was actually diminishing my message. I went from anger to gratitude. That lesson has influenced every session since. Criticism can be life changing.

Coping with criticism can be a challenge, but it's something we will all encounter at some time in our life. You can always transform a criticism from negative to a positive that you can use for your advantage. When you encounter criticism, remember to take a step back and think before you respond. This will give you a chance to see the positivity in every critique.

DIG DEEP:

Think back to a time when you received a critique. How did you handle it? What did you wish you could do over? What have you learned from past criticism? Did you survive the criticism? Did it make you stronger? How will you handle a critic from this day forward? Once you master this skill you will live a LifeAbundant365!

CHAPTER FIFTY-TWO:
Learning to Trust

EVERYBODY HAS EXPERIENCED THE PAIN of a broken trust. Trust is the foundation of all meaningful relationships. Once we stop trusting we wonder if we will ever be able to trust people again. Those experiences can be painful, and the feelings are completely normal. You cannot eliminate trust from your life. The good news is that you can trust again.

Personally, the biggest thing for me was to learn to trust myself again. I had always made good business decisions. However, there were a few projects where, in haste, I made poor choices. Those choices proved to be costly mistakes.

Putting trust in someone and then getting betrayed left me angry at the person, but angrier with myself. My negative self-talk sounded like, "How could I be so stupid? Why did I think this was a good idea?" On and on, I beat myself down for weeks. At one point I remember saying, "That will never happen again. I will never trust another business partner."

Over time, I remembered the three words that can change anyone's life: "Get – Over – It!" I knew I had to pick up the pieces and move forward. The first step was to Get – Over – It! To do that I had to forgive the person who broke my trust. I did. I began to take inventory of all the trusting relationships I had and of all the good choices I'd made. My good-trusting relationships far outweighed my bad ones. I began to trust myself again and I began to trust others. An old saying returned to me: "Trust is a fragile thing. Easy to break, easy to lose, and one of the hardest things to ever get back."

When we are operating on a "don't-trust" level, we lock out opportunities in our life. We become oblivious to everything around us. Not trusting will cause us to disengage with others for fear they will let us down. Eventually we place ourselves alone on our island. Distrust is a taught/learned behavior. You're not born distrustful. Your ability to trust others is directly related with your ability to trust yourself.

What happens when it's you that has broken or lost trust with someone? Something happened and you are now no longer trustworthy in the eyes of someone else. What's your next move to regain their confidence?

- Apologize where needed. This apology must be genuine and sincere in order to have an impact. The apology needs to include accountability and ownership over the actions that broke the trust.

- Be honest and consistent. If you broke the trust, the last thing you need is for the person you are trying to rebuild with observe behavior inconsistent with your apology. Words have power, but action will far exceed what you say. Arrive on time when you say you will be there. Call when you promised to call. Do what you say you will do. This is the building phase. Don't fail here.

- Rebuilding trust takes time, consistency, and patience. Your primary objective during this rebuilding is to be dependable, consistent, responsive, disciplined, and sensitive to the needs of others.

- Own it. Take full responsibility for the trust fracture and welcome being held accountable so it never happens again.

- Do nothing out of selfish ambition. It's not about you, even though it may be about what you have done.

Do nothing out of selfish ambition or vain conceit. Rather, in humility value others above yourselves, not looking to your own interests but each of you to the interests of the others. —Philippians 2:3-4 (NIV)

Trust can be rebuilt and become stronger than ever. However, in some cases, trust will never be the same. Regardless of what they or you do, the trust can't be rebuilt. At that point, you must accept that fact and honor it. Forgive where needed. Request forgiveness when appropriate. And then, just "Get – Over – It!" Time to move on so this situation doesn't define your future.

DIG DEEP:

Think back to when you have had a trust broken or when you broke a trust with someone else. What happened? Write the circumstance down in your journal. What have you done to trust again, or to regain the trust of someone else? Today is the day to get started on the path to trustworthy! Trust is the foundation for all relationships. Practice being trustworthy every day and watch your LifeAbundant365 flourish in your life.

CHAPTER FIFTY-THREE:
Generating the Best Ideas

COMING UP WITH GREAT IDEAS is the easy part. Ever see an idea that came together and wished you would have thought of it? Well, you can.

Taking action on great ideas is the difficult part.

Ideas primarily come from what we digest and what we've been exposed to the most. What you read, watch, and listen to are seeds for ideas. Good stuff in, good stuff out. We can't ingest junk and expect great ideas to develop. You don't plant jalapeno peppers and expect to harvest watermelons.

When I want to come up with a great idea, I'll go on a long run to free my mind from my normal stream of day-to-day thoughts. That shakes things up and allows me to gain another perspective. I've generated some of my best ideas while out on long runs.

Once I'd been out on such a long run and I found myself struggling. I couldn't understand why I couldn't stay on pace and complete a training run I had done hundreds of times in the past. Finally, I just quit thinking about the difficulties and let my mind wander. Then a powerful thought came to me: "Past performance doesn't guarantee future results." Sure, I had performed this training session many times in the past without difficulty, but that in no way meant such a session would always come easy. For me, I have to understand that from my neck up I'm thinking I'm thirty years old, but from the neck down my body is sixty years old. What I once did with ease now requires more effort and mindset.

The past is the past. We must perform at high levels now. We can't stand on the past because it has little impact on how we feel today. Every day presents a new opportunity. We must attack the day. When the future becomes the present is when you must give your best effort. Your past performance is your past performance. Enjoy your past successes and realize the struggle is real. Each day requires your very best.

Where do you get your best ideas?

Reading also generates ideas for me. I read about fifty books each year; last year I read sixty-three. This self-improvement escape is a fantastic way to get your brain humming. New territory abounds within each book. Reading opens your mind to new journeys and new ways to look at things. I've had many people tell me, "I'm not a good reader" or "I don't like to read." Okay, purchase an audiobook and let the book read itself to you. Even a few pages each day can get the idea generator running. Reading is the best way I know to self-improvement. The more I read, the better reader I become and the more I enjoy reading. Many new doors have been opened for me through reading more. I have developed friendships just by discussing a book I'd read. Learn to love to read.

Listen to podcasts and TED Talks. Our high-tech society provides so much information right at your fingertips. You can listen while you commute, work out, or in between meetings. Every topic you can think of is available to you. Kick-start your idea machine today by reading or listening. There is no limit to the great ideas you can generate. Self-limitations bring your only limitations.

Attend a conference or a seminar. Better yet, travel to a new location to attend an event. Being in a new venue will free you up to listen more and be less distracted than you would be at home. You will also meet new people, which leads to new friendships and relationships. New people will give you new ideas. Attend networking events and business meet-and-greet events. Practice what you learn and, most importantly, write down your new ideas as you think of them. Don't trust your memory to save the idea. Many great ideas are lost in the memory-maze. Capture every idea—good or bad—and sort them out later. Don't just think it, ink it!

So, you have this incredible idea, now what? How do you move forward and take action?

Step 1: Select the best idea to work on.

Step 2: Find a mentor or business partner with experience in this new idea. The need here is accountability to keep moving forward.

Step 3: Develop an action plan to follow. Remember these are always going to change once you start. The key is to start.

Step 4: Take baby steps. One step at a time is the best plan here. Just take the next logical step.

Step 5: Evaluate. Keep learning and improving on your great idea. Your idea could become the biggest thing that's ever happened to you. Again, accountability is critical.

Step 6: Adapt and improve. Make the changes as they become evident. This can happen several times in the process.

Step 7: Stay enthusiastic about your idea. This requires discipline.

Step 8: When your idea is a success, don't stop. It's just the beginning to what you can accomplish.

Step 9: Become the self-disrupter. Don't get comfortable with your success. There are other folks coming up with an idea that will make yours obsolete. You be the one to come up with what's next. Keep thinking and keep generating great ideas.

DIG DEEP:

What was the last great idea you had? How did you come up with the idea? How much time are you investing in your future? What does that plan look like? Take some of the ideas in this chapter for generating new ideas and implement them today! These new great ideas with have you living a LifeAbundant365.

CHAPTER FIFTY-FOUR:
Burn Your Boats!

WE'VE ALL HEARD THE STORY about Spanish conquistador Hernán Cortés, who issued a bizarre order to his six hundred men as they began their conquest of the Aztec empire in 1519: "Burn the boats!"

They were outnumbered by the Aztecs 100-1 and many had tried and failed to conquer the Aztec empire. Something new needed to be attempted. A drastic measure to increase their odds of winning while being outnumbered.

"Burn the boats!" Cortés wanted his men to know that retreating was not an option. Fighting with everything they had was their only course of action because losing would bring dire consequences. That made winning this battle the most important thing to Cortés's men and they focused accordingly. Win or die, no other options.

I've read or heard versions about "Burn the boats!" Some say it never happened. Some say they sunk the boats and didn't burn them. Many other variations of the tale exist. Regardless, the message I took away from the story was this: Retreating or quitting is easy when it's an option.

Many of us operate our lives based on fear. We'll postpone an action until we no longer fear something that may or may not happen. Allowing fear and feelings to guide your life makes for a miserable existence.

During the last five years I have spoken to thousands of attendees at my events. Hundreds have told me, "I wish." "I can't." "I never." "I would love to." Pick one to fill in the blank. I'll say, "Oh really, tell me about all of the attempts and things you have tried and failed at." And "How long have you been trying?"

"None" is usually their answer! They haven't even tried.

The secret I share is that they aren't going through something, they are growing through it. They just need to go all in!

"Burn the boats!"

What boats do you need to burn in your life right now? Where are you hanging on to something that's diminishing to you and your life conditions? What safety net or training wheels do you need to remove right now? Having a Plan B for escape when things get difficult usually leads to settling or quitting.

To grow and succeed in any area of your life, you must commit to the mindset that failure is not an option—that you have no boat to retreat to. If you always have a Plan B, you have already failed at some level. If retreating is not an option, you will get up every morning, make decisions, and take action. You are all in and no other options exist besides winning. All of your thoughts and efforts will be pointed to succeeding in this one commitment in your life.

I've seen many wannabe real estate agents holding on to their other jobs while trying to set up new real estate practices. To me, this represents a lack of faith in their own abilities, commitment, and their belief that they can succeed in the industry. They believe if they hold on to a lifeline, they will be saved if they can't do it. Instead, they are diminishing their opportunity to succeed. They also diminish their value in their position because their focus is divided.

We have been programmed to accept a mentality of "this is how we do it" or "this is the way we've always done it." Go to school, get a job, get married, get a mortgage, and save money for retirement. If you have saved enough money and are healthy, you can then travel some or enjoy your golden years after you retire. If this represents total success for you, then you have already burned your boats in a sense. If this is not your idea of success, you need to burn your boats and win at your dreams and passion.

All change happens first with a thought, then a decision, and finally a commitment to change. You may want change your body, eliminate debt, start a new career, or finish your education. After you make your decision to change, the most critical step is to change the action you take to make the change happen. Make a commitment decision—one you can't go back on because you are all in—then totally surrender to making that decision do what you decided for it to do. Few of us reach this level of commitment, but for those special few who do, they not only change their lives, they change the lives of their family and community. All because they decided to "Burn the boats!"

If you really want it, burn your boats and get going.

DIG DEEP:

Where in your life do you need a fresh start? What dream, or purpose, are you willing to fully commit to? What boats must you burn to ensure you will not turn back? When will you take the first step toward your dreams and start living a LifeAbundant365?

CHAPTER FIFTY-FIVE:
Success at Every Age

IT'S NEVER TOO LATE to make a difference in your life and the lives of others. Every season brings new opportunities as well as a different perspective. Never stop learning and growing at any age.

When I was young, I heard the following statement countless times: "When you have your health, you have everything!"

Still, I never understood the truth in that thought.

My adult life has always been full of running, exercising, and playing sports. I've been through obstacle courses, marathons, ultramarathons, and other endurance sports and, for the most part, I've always been in good health.

Fast-forward to when I turned sixty. I experienced a torn Achilles tendon, a heel spur, and plantar fasciitis. After many appointments with physicians and surgeons, followed by weeks of physical therapy, I began to think that when you lose your health, you lose yourself. Months and months of not exercising—and especially not running— left me discouraged and frustrated. The physicians and therapists kept reminding me that I wasn't as young as I used to be, so the process of healing took longer.

When you have your health, you have everything!

Practice good health practices. Try to eat right and get in the habit of moving more.

Everyone is on their own schedule. Some want to retire young while others never want to retire. Some want stay active while others are too old and ... you get the idea. Stop trying to compare yourself to others.

Everyone is wired differently. Work your own plan. Just because someone didn't plan ahead, and now they're in a hurry, doesn't mean you have to be. It's one thing to be accommodating and yet another to be tossed around here and there because others failed to prepare. Craft a plan for the rest of your life and execute that plan. Don't let others force you off your plan.

Never settle. I have a business friend that has settled his entire life. He told me he'd never bought a new car. He's never bought name brands, just generic versions for food, medicine, electronics, clothes, appliances, etc. To him, name brands were too expensive. He and his wife only traveled for work or if they could avoid hotel costs by staying with relatives. He's told me about places he would have loved to have seen, things he wanted to experience, and things he wished he had done earlier in his life when he had the opportunities. Now he thinks he is too old, or it's too late for him.

I understand and agree with being smart with your money. However, you can't allow the fear of not having enough keep you from experiencing life. The trips I've taken with my family have been expensive, but the memories are priceless. Don't settle for less in every area of your life. You deserve more.

Become grateful for everything. Showing gratitude isn't so much about what we say—although that's a part of it—it's more about how we live. Be grateful for the smallest things and you will show gratitude for the major things in life. Stop being a consumer and begin being a first-class contributor. Your life begins when you assist others with their needs. The more you give, the more you get. It's true. Life is fleeting, so why not enjoy every day?

Be yourself. Never try to live up to others' expectations of who you should be or what you should do. Everyone has an idea for your life and most of them mean well. The problem is their expectations don't usually match your dream or your plan. Just be yourself. Only you know what excites and satisfies you. Focus all of your energy and effort on your desires. Don't waste energy listening to those who want to change you. Be authentic.

Life is a journey to be enjoyed. While I'll admit that not every day of my life has been a joy, I can see that every day has been a journey. Journeys are to be enjoyed. Allow yourself to look around and see the people you love and the things that bring you true joy. You can then begin to appreciate your journey. Once I learned the value of the journey, I began to see life in a different way. No matter how good or how bad your current situation is, it will change. Don't fret about the small stuff, change is coming. We are but a vapor—here today and gone tomorrow. Enjoy and embrace the present. For now, it's all we have.

Believe in yourself. Many people will treat you by the way you present yourself. Your confidence or lack of confidence will shine through every time. Remember, you get to set your standard of how you want to be treated. If you don't, others will treat you the way they want to treat you. Raise your standard. If you don't love yourself, don't expect others to love you either.

Change. If we change, the world will change. The world is a reflection of who we really are on the inside. If you are complaining about how evil, or greedy, or selfish the world is today, begin a change within you. In as little as a few weeks, you could notice a difference in the world because there is a difference in you.

"We cannot become what we need by remaining what we are."
—*John C. Maxwell*

DIG DEEP:

Our lives are in constant change.

"Change is inevitable. Growth is optional." —*John C. Maxwell*

What big new thing do you want to achieve in this season of your life? Where in your life do you need to grow? When you grow, you add value to the people and community around you. Without growth you have nothing to give because you can't give what you don't have. Where in this season can you serve? This is LifeAbundant365.

DON DAY is a motivational speaker at dondaySpeaks, a company specializing in the Whole Person Concept training of individuals, groups and organizations. He is also a top-selling realtor, author of *The Surge Effect*, and coach. Don's sessions build champions. Day is a husband of one, a father of two, and a grandfather of four.

CPSIA information can be obtained
at www.ICGtesting.com
Printed in the USA
JSHW011559100120
3503JS00001B/2

9 780578 560403